TOUCHED BY ANGELS OF MERCY

TOUCHED BY ANGELS OF MERCY

*small doses of genuine life by
nurses, patients and caregivers*

Laura Lagana, RN

To order additional copies of this book, contact:
Xlibris Corporation
1-888-7-XLIBRIS
www.Xlibris.com
Orders@Xlibris.com

WHAT OTHERS HAVE REVEALED ABOUT TOUCHED BY ANGELS OF MERCY

"Insightful vignettes of nurse heroism that makes one proud to be a nurse. This book is enlightening–the heart and soul of caring reflected by stories of nurses and how they made a difference. . . . a big difference. I am blessed to be a nurse."

Laura Gasparis Vonfrolio RN, PhD, CEN
president, Education Enterprises
president, Power-Publications
author, publisher, lecturer and consultant
New York

"Nurses are very special people and these touching stories and poems demonstrate that aspect of nursing with much dignity and grace. Many will benefit from the accounts you share . . . "

Linda Morrison Combs Ed. D.
consultant, professional speaker
author of *A Long Goodbye and Beyond*
North Carolina

"These are the beautiful and often untold stories of the sacredness and joy of everyday life for a caregiver. A must read for anyone who is a nurse by profession or by duty; or has ever considered being a nurse; or anyone who has ever encountered an angel of mercy.

Donna Cardillo, RN
president, Cardillo & Associates
New Jersey

"This reinforces the fact that we never know who God will send into our lives to be our special angel. A beautiful and touching reminder of the need for faith and perseverance."

Jackie Kucera
caregiver and wife of a cancer patient
Wisconsin

"Ms. Lagana presents what many people know but few articulate: the caring, genuine concern for humanity that is nursing, undergirded by a sound knowledge base. These stories deliver the message in a most human and personal way."

Karen Morin, DSN, RN
professor of nursing, Penn State University
Pennsylvania

"It's been a joy reading these stories and poems about real angels on earth."

Claire Letourneaux, RD
registered dietitian, St. Paul Home Inc.
Wisconsin

"Nurses and caregivers will appreciate this collection of inspirational and spiritual connection for those who deal with illness or those who need help. The stories and poems relate how certain situations, considered by many to be sad and futile, may provide an opportunity for hope and joy to those who choose this life of giving."

Jean Raymond, MS, RN
geriatric/gerontological clinical nurse specialist
Delaware

"As I read the stories, I found myself experiencing a profound respect and appreciation for the angels we call nurses. These men and women give much of themselves emotionally, physically and spiritually. This collection reflects a deep sense of commitment and love. You will be inspired and grateful that these people have chosen nursing; for at some time in our lives we, or someone we love, will be faced with a medical crisis. Fortunately, there will be people like the ones described in these stories available to support our healing.

Esther Wright, M.A.
educator, author of *Why I Teach*
California

"This wonderful collection of heartwarming and uplifting stories reminds us of what a noble profession it is to serve others through the skillful practice and loving art of nursing."

Jack Canfield
co-author, *Chicken Soup for the Soul*
California

"As a registered nurse, I have always been proud of my profession. This book reinforces that pride. In these stories we see beyond the theory and technology; we see love, tenderness and compassion."

Helen Daley, RN
geriatric nurse
Delaware

This book is dedicated to God, all nurses and caregivers, patients and their families, friends and significant others, and Angels of Mercy everywhere who take care of, or who have ever taken care of, another person.

CONTENTS

ACKNOWLEDGMENTS

Many people have generously shared their time, expertise, and occasionally their tears, to help make this book possible. My heartfelt thanks and gratitude to all, especially:

Tom, my loving soul-mate, best friend, business partner, mentor, computer consultant and jack-of-all-trades, for your gifts of love, inspiration, patience, humor and support. Our precious sons, Brandon and Daniel, our daughter-in-law, Jackie, and our grandson, Brandon, for your steadfast love, e-mail messages, telephone calls and welcome words of encouragement. Linda, my sister and good friend, for patiently tolerating my countless shenanigans over the years and for listening with an open heart. My steadfast parents, Lucille Shreatte and Melville Hayes, for nurturing my passion for writing and answering endless questions. May you continue to enjoy heavenly bliss together.

Jack Canfield, co-author of *Chicken Soup for the Soul*, for your generous words of inspiration that awakened my slumbering passion for writing, and for reading my initial manuscript.

Echo Heron, nurse-author and mindful mentor, for your guidance, valuable suggestions and constructive candor.

Nursing Spectrum, for your role in sharing the "call for stories." Bob Hess, for publishing my first story. Cindy Saver, for encouraging me to continue writing. Carrie Farella, nurse journalist, for your persistent enthusiasm and constructive comments.

Paula Schneider and LeAnn Thieman, for generously sharing your expertise while working on your own books.

Abigail Scott, of *Advance for Nurses*, for your informative interview and keen interest.

Matt Matteo, who generously gave of his time and talent to add the element of humor through his cartoons.

My nursing instructors, professors, classmates and dorm-buddies, former patients and their families, colleagues and all who have touched my life, for teaching me far more than you will ever know.

All of the authors who sent their stories, poems and artwork, for sharing your touching, personal experiences and momentous memories. I only wish that all of your works could have been included.

The assiduous readers, for volunteering your time and talent to patiently read and assess each story: Jeanne Alford, RN; Laura Allen; Neil Soriano Bagadiong; Shirley Becker; Candace Campbell, PA-C; Judy Cook, RN; June Curti, RN, BSN; Susilee Dean, RN; Shirley Doan; Lynn Durham, RN; Normandie Fallon, RN; Carrie Farella, RN, MA; Judith Friedman; Lana Robertson Hayes; Theresa Hommel, RN, BSN; Donna and Hal Jacobs; Jackie Kucera; Charlotte Lafean, RNC, BSN; Catherine Lagana, RN; Jacqueline Lagana; Tom Lagana; Claire Letourneaux, RD; Judy Magnon, RN,c., BS, LADC; Rene' Maldonado; Linda and Bob Pyle; Rosemarie Riley; Debra Skelly, RN, BSN, CPN; Judy Triziski; Monica Troy; Jack Vaughn; and Cindy Wilhite, RN. Although some readers were inspired to submit their own work, none of the contributing authors rated their own material.

I am sincerely grateful to all who have shared their esteemed guidance, wisdom and loving support.

INTRODUCTION

Blessed with the burning desire to write, I began keeping a diary as soon as I learned how to print. Early childhood memories include my father's creative writing and speech lessons where my sister, Linda, and I reviewed vocabulary and took turns reading aloud from the *Reader's Digest*. Years later, I grew to appreciate my father's gifts, and my diary eventually became my journal.

I was also born with the desire to help, to heal and to love—both people and animals. I tried to fix injured birds, coaxed stray cats and dogs to follow me home and conducted many fish and turtle funerals. When I discovered it wasn't always possible to help or to heal, I knew I could still love, pray and hope.

At the age of five, while my parents picnicked on the beach, I nearly drowned in Lake Michigan. My sister summoned help, saving my life. The incredible feeling of peace, as I bobbed up and down with the waves, felt natural and peaceful. In a childish way, I faced the likelihood of my own death.

In the first year of my nursing education, I cared for two patients who vividly described their after-death experiences. The realistic details of their encounters made a lasting impression on me.

Two years later, while swimming at the New Jersey seashore, I was caught in a rip-tide. My boyfriend managed to grab hold of my arm despite the murky, sandy water. Fortunately, he saved my life before I was pulled out to sea. At the age of twenty, this served as yet another reminder of my own mortality.

While working as a newly-graduated nurse on a psychiatric ward, my young female patient attempted to strangle me. I felt grateful to be alive and had an even greater respect for the precious gift of life.

In August 1969, I graduated as a nurse. Along the way, I helped many people to heal and prayed with those who couldn't. I nursed two sick sons and a husband back to health, and buried both of my parents and my father-in-law. I also learned that there are no coincidences in this incredible journey called "life."

Three events inspired me to begin working on this book. The first was Christopher Reeve's equestrian accident on May 27, 1995. This astounding man courageously turned an unexpected, negative life-experience into an opportunity to make a positive difference in many lives that were shattered by spinal cord injuries.

The second, less dramatic but very significant, event was saying *yes* to my husband's request that we attend a seminar together in California, in July of 1997. Although we didn't know what to expect, we went to Jack Canfield's Facilitation Skills Seminar. After participating in the interactive exercises of that action-packed, life-altering week, I rediscovered my life-long passion for writing.

The third event was the sudden death of Princess Diana on August 30, 1997. This kind-hearted young woman and mother, who had touched many lives worldwide, was suddenly killed in a tragic automobile accident. How ironic that Mother Teresa followed her in death, only days later.

In December 1997, the idea for *Touched by Angels of Mercy* was born, and I began writing and collecting short stories and poems. In the process of reading hundreds of letters, poems and stories that were submitted, two things became crystal-clear to me: that people have the need and desire to share their experiences with others; and this sharing process is often healthful and therapeutic.

As a nurse, mother, intermittent caregiver and occasional patient, I understand how important it is to consider the whole person—the physical, mental, emotional and spiritual aspects. This holistic approach is clearly an effective way to diagnose and deal with illness, whether to achieve the state of wellness or to ease the process of dying.

In addition, the growing number of caregivers often feel apprehensive, exhausted, overwhelmed and isolated; they desperately need relief and support too. The need to be touched by another and to recount personal experiences are universal human requirements. The strength, knowledge and inspiration that comes from sharing personal life and death experiences with one another stimulates healing. Wounds heal from the inside out—so does the heart and soul.

Nursing offers a multitude of unique moments to make a difference in the lives of others, as well as in our own. Many nurses, patients and caregivers have had at least one special moment to cherish forever.

As nursing continues to evolve and the scope of practice widens, it is important to remember those from our past who have been instrumental in shaping the nursing profession, as well as our world.

Since volumes have already been written on the historical aspects of nursing and caregiving, I have selected two extraordinary people who have earned a distinguished place in history, for consideration in this book.

Florence Nightingale, "The Founder of Modern Nursing," dedicated her life to ministering to the sick. During the Crimean War, she organized a group of nurses to aid the wounded and later established the first school designed to train nurses in London in 1860. Florence Nightingale elevated nursing to a profession.

Clara Barton, (Clarissa Harlowe Barton), was nicknamed "The Angel of the Battlefield" because of her dedication to the injured during the Civil War. She eventually was named superintendent of the Union nurses. In 1881 she was instrumental in organizing the American Red Cross.

The profession of nursing deals with the prevention of illness and the care and rehabilitation of the sick. It takes a special person to answer this "calling." The word "angel" comes from the Greek word meaning *—angelos—* messenger. Since angels are God's messengers, it's no small wonder that nurses are sometimes referred to as "angels of mercy."

Today's nurses are vastly different from those of yesteryear.

-LAGA

Although the changing world of healthcare has created many challenges for nursing, it has also brought new frontiers. Change will always be a part of our lives; and likewise, our need to be touched by one another and to share common experiences.

For nurses, the goal remains the same—to make a difference in the lives of their patients. Nurses and caregivers reach out and become "angels" for others. They are compassionate, intelligent and caring beings that provide hands-on care, to help the sick to heal, or comfort them as they die. Nurses and caregivers are not invincible; they also need to take care of *themselves*.

There are many in this world who might be labeled as "angels of mercy." This term is not limited solely to nurses, however. Our world needs the healing "angels" who come to us in a variety of forms, when and where we least expect them.

Except for a few cases where permission has been granted, fictitious names have been substituted for actual names, in order to protect confidentiality and respect anonymity.

Writing these stories has been a therapeutic experience for our authors, and for some, an extremely difficult task. We invite you to contact the authors, and to peruse the resource information that is provided within these pages. It is our hope that, by reading and sharing these real-life, personal experiences, you too will be touched, inspired and healed.

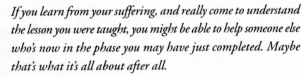

If you learn from your suffering, and really come to understand the lesson you were taught, you might be able to help someone else who's now in the phase you may have just completed. Maybe that's what it's all about after all.

~ Anonymous

CHAPTER 1
THE POWER OF LOVE

One word frees us of all the weight and pain of life: that word is love.

~ Sophocles

In the Arms of Angels

I glanced at the clock on the musty green hospital wall. Almost midnight. *Had it really been only twenty-one hours since the ringing phone startled me from sleep, spinning* my life *out of control?* Panicked, I grabbed the receiver, fearing something had happened to my mother. But it was my mother's voice I heard on the other end: "Your younger sister . . . Rondi . . . brain aneurysm . . . coma . . . surgery . . . can you fly to New York right away?"

Before I knew it, I was pacing in an intensive care unit waiting room. The walls, supposedly painted to look soft and welcoming, instead felt cold and threatening. Random chairs sat scattered, while others formed small circles of comfort for families. This room was like no place else on earth. Time stood still here.

I walked to the window and gazed from the eighth floor at the people below. I wanted to scream, *How dare you have the audacity to carry on normal lives! Don't you have any idea what's happening up here?*

Yes, my world had definitely stopped. On one side of the waiting room, where we'd "made camp," friends and relatives congregated to pray, help, cry, ask why and bring food. It felt like we should be gathering for a party, not pleading for Rondi to make it through the night.

Family members were allowed in her room, only one or two at

a time. We "took shifts" around the clock so Rondi would never be alone. I walked in, startled by the incongruity of seeing her peacefully asleep, quiet, no movement amidst the chaotic activity around her. I counted the rhythmic sounds from monitors and machines—the eerie whoosh of the ventilator and the steady "beep-beep" proving she was still alive.

Nurses, dressed in blue, bustled around checking lines, gauges and tubing, as if Rondi was the only patient in the whole hospital. I retreated to the background, afraid to sit in a chair that would be in the way or ask bothersome questions. Then I noticed. All these nurse's faces reflected knowledge, determination and purpose, yet in their eyes I saw softness and patience. I marveled at the realization that Rondi's very life rested in the hands of these souls, and God.

I had the midnight to 4 a.m. shift. It was 1:56 a.m. Things in the room became quieter as only one nurse cared for Rondi. Through misty eyes, I read her name—Linda. The flurry calmed as she dimmed the lights and the machines echoed their discordant beats. Now I had time to think and feel helpless, with no control. I could do nothing to make my sister better.

With tubes and wires all over her, I didn't even know where it was safe to touch her. And how I yearned to touch her, so she'd know I was there, wanting to help. I would do anything, but I had no idea what that should be. If all the medicine, machines and beeping couldn't save her, then what on earth could I do? The frustration welled up inside me as the tears finally let go. I felt so alone.

I gleaned a bit of comfort as I watched the nurse check Rondi's monitor connections with the gentlest touch. Sure, she was performing the tasks necessary to save a life, but there was more. She smiled at Rondi while she worked and talked softly to her, even though she was in a coma. How I wished I could connect with Rondi in such an intimate way.

Suddenly I noticed the nurse was talking to me, too. Carefully lifting sections of Rondi's hair, she commented on how sad it was that bedrest caused it to become so mercilessly matted.

Then, out of the blue she looked to me. "Do you have a brush?"

Numbly, I retrieved one from my purse. She motioned me to the head of the bed and gently showed me how to brush small sections of Rondi's hair and lay them on the pillow without disturbing any tubes or wires. My little sister's hair felt so light in my hand as I touched her for the first time. I was helping, actually doing something to care for her. The nurse dimmed the lights and quietly slipped out of the room, but not before she smiled again, this time at me.

I felt like Rondi and I were the only two people in the world during the hour I brushed her hair. That precious time meant more to me than any other hour we had ever spent together. With the lights lowered, I talked to her, hoping in an odd way that she would open her eyes and tell me she was going to be fine. But I knew she couldn't do that. If only I could know she was safe and not feeling any pain. As I brushed, I lamented about where people "went" during comas.

As if to answer my questions, a new sound emerged past the hospital noises—music. It must have been playing in the background all the time, but I hadn't heard it before this. From the chorus of her beautiful song, "Angels," I caught the familiar strains of Sarah McLachlan's song. Yes! I knew at that moment where Rondi was. She was safe, not in pain, being cared for by angels until it was time for her to return to us here in this room.

It's hard to describe the power and beauty of the moment Rondi's nurse insightfully created for us that night. *Did she know?* After all, she ministers to patients every day, nonstop, during her shifts. It's her job, and this could be just an everyday activity for her, but it meant the world to me. I'm in awe to think that if only one person a week is the recipient of her gift, imagine how many lives she has changed in her twenty-plus years "on the job."

That morning, at 1:56 a.m., there was a great deal of healing that needed to take place in that room. This wise, wonderful nurse saw that and nurtured it. Rondi was in the arms of more than one angel that night. We both were.

by Elaine Gray Dumler

Elaine Gray Dumler is a professional speaker and author. She specializes in helping people learn how to talk to each other better through networking and presentation skill training. She travels internationally, and has been a guest on radio and television. As evidenced by her story, 1999 brought many challenges. Elaine learned to prioritize an "out of control" life. She can be reached at (303) 430-0592; e-mail: FraklySpkg@aol.com.

Just a Hug

*We need four hugs a day for survival. We need eight hugs a day
for maintenance. We need twelve hugs a day for growth.*

~ Virginia Satir

Morning report included a new patient who had been admitted
during the evening shift with a diagnosis of a CVA (cerebrovascular
accident or stroke). Eighty-one-year-old Mr. Eagen was not only
aphasic (having partial or complete loss of the ability to verbalize
ideas or comprehend spoken or written language), but was also
described as being wild and sexually aggressive. The night staff
related they had found it necessary to restrain him with a soft
waist belt to keep him in bed and hand restraints to keep him
from pawing them.

As I made out the day's assignment I wondered how I, as charge
nurse and oldest staff member, was going to handle this man in a
way which would help our younger staff nurses to provide care to
this patient.

On rounds, a few minutes later, I entered the room directly
opposite the nurse's station. I found a tall, robust, elderly
gentleman, with a sweet, baby face and thinning white hair, lying
rigid on his bed, well-restrained. He turned to me as I approached
and began straining as he reached out to me. He quieted as I said,
"Good morning."

I opened the draperies and took one restrained hand in mine.
Breakfast trays were arriving in the rooms and I gingerly released
one hand, then the other, to see if he could feed himself. He didn't
seem to know what to do with the utensils or food, so I fed him,
remaining cautiously out of reach of those notorious hands, keeping
the over-bed table between us. Once he was finished with the
meal I loosely restrained his hands once again.

A few minutes later Mrs. Eagen arrived looking delicate and
frail, quite a contrast to her husband's strong and hearty appearance.

She was an emotional basket-case and seemed as bewildered and confused as her husband. Over the next few minutes, she was noticeably tearful. When I explained that her husband couldn't speak to her or appear to understand any of us, she became even more distraught. I treated her to some juice, crackers and conversation in the cafeteria.

From our conversation I learned that, until the previous evening, Mr. Eagen had been the total authority and mainstay of their household. At eighty-one he still ran his own successful business, paid the bills, managed the finances including balancing the checkbook, decided on major purchases, home repairs and improvements. Throughout their fifty-five years of marriage, Mrs. Eagen had been content with their respective roles—that of confident, capable caretaker and cherished, sheltered wife. As she talked, it became apparent she had no idea how to handle things by herself.

When she finished, what clearly was her breakfast, we returned to Mr. Eagen. I invited her to stay as I gave morning care. The interaction between them seemed to indicate a great deal of closeness and interdependency. Mr. Eagen kept looking toward her while I worked and talked to both of them. He was calm and cooperative until I finished his bath, when he suddenly grabbed me. My first thought was, *Oh no, not in front of his wife!*

In an effort to cover his actions, I reached for him and gave him a big hug. Almost immediately the confusion and despair dissipated from his face and he relaxed again with a broad smile. It dawned on me that his so-called sexual aggression was only an inner need to be hugged.

I suggested to the other staff that when he became agitated and "grabby," we return his gestures with a hug. They all agreed to try it. Mrs. Eagen was informed of our plan and readily gave her permission. Over the next few days he became the unit's beloved grandpa and there was no more need to restrain his hands. "Hug Therapy" was permanently incorporated into his plan of care.

In the interim, I contacted the hospital chaplain who was able to spend ample time talking with Mrs. Eagen; something we didn't have time to do ourselves on our busy unit. Rehabilitation services, primarily speech and occupational therapy, were enlisted to begin the long, slow process of reorientation, safety training and retraining of the activities of daily living.

The most important contact was with social services, who worked with Mrs. Eagen to teach her the art of home management. Over the next several weeks she began to realize the scope of the role-reversal that was taking place. Mrs. Eagen was so grateful for all the coaching and counseling that she would burst into tears whenever she attempted to express gratitude. It wasn't long until the tears turned into smiles when she realized she could run the household.

Mr. Eagen had no paralysis but he had lost a great deal of mental function, including speech, judgment and sense of balance. He couldn't be left unattended unless he had a waist restraint in place; but he would happily accept a trip to the bathroom, a walk down the hall with the support of two people, or a short visit in a geriatric chair at the nurse's station so he could watch the activity. He beamed at all of us, accepting and giving hugs freely.

Some say, "Don't get emotionally involved with a patient." But the hugs and the emotional involvement made all the difference to this special couple, and were the deciding factors in their care. Mr. Eagen was finally transferred to the rehab unit for an extended stay where both he and his wife continued to receive the practical and medical care we started.

Mr. Eagen has experienced several more hospitalizations since his CVA. Both he and his wife always stop to visit on their way to therapy or testing. On each visit, I always get a hug. After each visit I watch them walk down the hall together—an elderly couple holding hands—a confident, capable caretaker and her cherished, sheltered husband.

by Charlotte Iliff Lafean

Charlotte Iliff Lafean, RNC, BSN, is retired from full-time nursing, and is self-employed on a part-time basis as substitute school nurse, home-health aide instructor and insurance examiner. She loved her nursing career, the reason she continues to dabble in nursing related areas. She can be reached at P.O. Box 1115, Mcafee, NJ 07428; Telephone: (973) 209-4077.

THE DEEP END by Matt Matteo

Reprinted by permission of Matt Matteo.
THE DEEP END Cartoons by Matt Matteo
Matt Matteo is an award-winning artist, author of two cartoon series, book illustrator and adult tutor from Derry, Pennsylvania. He contributes much of his work to benefit charities and can be reached at BS-7345, 801 Butler Pike, Mercer, PA 16137.

The Healing Power of Mom's Milk Toast

Her name wasn't Florence Nightingale, and she wasn't a real nurse, but to me, Mom was the world's greatest nurse. She knew things beyond "doctoring" to make you feel better. It is a wonder I wasn't sick all the time. You really got a lot of attention at my house when you were sick. Tapioca pudding, chicken noodle soup and milk toast.

Oh come on, you mean your mother never fixed you milk toast when you had that horrible sore throat and couldn't swallow? Well, let me tell you about milk toast.

It takes a lot of tender loving care to make milk toast. First, you toast the bread and butter it. Then you cut it up into little bite-size squares, sprinkle sugar on it and pour scalded warm milk over it. The toast soaks up the warm milk, the yellow butter flakes float to the top, and the sugar sweetens it all. It slides right over swollen tonsils. It soothes the raw burning sensation that makes you think you are going to die; or at the very least, never swallow again.

And that's not all. While you are sitting in a chair, slowly swallowing your breakfast to make the good feelings last, she straightens your sheets. Turned-back covers and fluffed pillows leave a beautiful invitation for a morning nap to sleep the pain away.

When you awaken, she is there with a cool wash rag to bathe your hot, flushed face. Your temperature always goes up when you are sleeping. Next, she patiently mashes an aspirin and mixes it with sugar because it hurts too bad to swallow a whole one. A bowl of strawberry-flavored gelatin follows the bitter aspirin experience. Vanilla cookies on the side tempt you to swallow.

Guess what happened while you were on your trip to the bathroom? (The trips are frequent from all the juice and liquids.) The sheets were magically straightened, covers folded back and pillows fluffed. The sheets seemed cooler and more inviting every time she did that, which was whenever you left the bed for an instant. It was hard to catch her doing it. Sometimes you begin to wonder if you left it that way. No, your hot body constantly wiggled, seeking a cool spot to put out the fire. Sometimes mom's have invisible qualities.

I never figured out when she took care of her other chores. She was always there when I needed her. She brought me comic books and would sit and read from *Heidi* or *Alice In Wonderland,* but only one chapter at a time. I guess I slept longer than I thought. She always knew when to poke her head around the corner so I wouldn't have to yell or beat on the floor for attention. It hurt too much to talk, much less yell.

I often wondered, *Do kids ever die from sore throats?* When you start wondering things like that, you want your mother nearby. Mine was always there with a special treat to make me feel better. Blessed assurance that I wasn't going to die.

I wonder, *If my mom hadn't been a Mom, would she have been a nurse?* She always knew how to make me feel better. *My mom, a nurse?* No, she couldn't have been a nurse. She didn't have nurse's training. Besides, she was too busy being my mom, making tapioca pudding, milk toast and chicken noodle soup, fluffing pillows and reading books. No, she was "just-a-mom," a loving Mom.

by Perry Arledge-Smith

Perry Arledge-Smith (Perry A~) is a keynote speaker, author and facilitator. Her defining statement is: "Touching people with their own greatness." She can be reached at P.O. Box 152139 Austin, TX 78715; Telephone: (512) 441-0335; Fax: (512) 441-0206; e-mail: srewards@aol.com; Web site: http://www.perrya.com.

One More Kiss from Rose

Often we waste so much energy with what was or what will be that we have little time left for what is.

~ Dr. Leo Buscaglia

Mr. Kenney returned to our unit of the hospital frequently. He was a retired executive, a widower, and cancer had taken took its toll over the last three years. The cancer had metastasized from his colon to all of his vital organs. This would probably be his last admission, and I believe he knew it.

Some patients are known to be "problems" because of behavior changes that often accompany major diseases. When people are suffering they aren't aware of what they say or do to people, and frequently they lash out at the first person that enters their room.

All things considered, every nurse is well aware of these circumstances. The more experienced nurses have acquired knowledge in how to handle such cases. Of course, this is where I come in—the "new kid" on the block, in a manner of speaking.

For days the other nurses would talk about Mr. Kenney at report, and there were special staff meetings to decide how to handle his outrageous behavior. Everyone tried to spend as little time as possible while in his room. Sometimes he threw things at the nurses and other staff members if they so much as looked at him the wrong way.

One evening, while on a particularly busy shift, we had more than our share of emergency admissions on the already overcrowded medical-surgical unit. Mr. Kenney picked this same evening to refuse his medications and decided to throw every large object that was well within his reach, while cursing at the top of his lungs. I could hardly believe that a terminally ill man of eighty-one could reach that volume and cause so much damage.

While I cautiously entered his room, I started talking. "What can I do for you, Mr. Kenney? What seems to be the problem?

There is such a ruckus in here that even the visitors are terrified. I don't know what to think of it. The other patients are trying to get to sleep."

An annoyed Mr. Kenney put down his next projectile (that seemed to be aimed at me) and asked me to sit in the chair next to his bed for a minute. Knowing I didn't really have the time, I still said, "Okay."

As I sat on the edge of the chair, Mr. Kenney proceeded to share some of his life with me. He started by saying, "No one understands how hard it is. How long it has been since I felt well. It has been so long since . . . since . . . anyone has even taken the time to really look at me, to listen to me . . . and to care."

A long silence followed and I wondered if this wouldn't be the best time to politely leave, but I didn't have the heart. Something told me to stay with this man.

After what seemed like an hour, he finally said, "It has been so long since I have had my Rose with me. My lovely, sweet Rose. We would always kiss goodnight, and that made everything better. No matter what happened that day, Rose's kisses always made everything better. Oh, God, how I would give anything for one more kiss from Rose." Then Mr. Kenney started crying.

He held onto my hand and said, "I know you must think I'm crazy, but I know my life is almost over. I look forward to being with my Rose again. My life is hell this way! I really appreciate your taking the time to listen—to really listen to me. I know you are terribly busy. I know you care."

"I don't mind at all. While I prepare to give you your medication, is there anything else that I can do for you?"

"Please, call me Joseph," he said as he rolled over very cooperatively. I gave him his injections and he thought for a few moments before answering my question. As I was almost finished, he finally said, "There is one last favor you could do for me."

"What is it, Joseph?" I asked.

Then he leaned over the side of the bed, and said in a hushed voice, "Could you just give me a goodnight kiss? Rose's kisses always made everything better. Could you just give me a kiss goodnight? Please? Oh, God, how I would give anything for one more kiss from Rose."

So I did. I walked over and placed a huge kiss on his cheek. It felt right to kiss a dying man in the place of his "Rose."

During report the next day, the nurses said Mr. Kenney had slipped peacefully away during the night. It is wonderful to know how strong true love can be–to be inseparable even after death. I was so honored that Mr. Kenney asked me to give him one more kiss from Rose.

by Laura Lagana, RN

A Mother's Commitment

Angeles is an alert, elderly woman of ninety-one, who resides in a nursing center. She is crippled with arthritis and osteoporosis, and confined to a wheelchair and a bed. Her skin is soft and silky smooth, much like a baby's behind; but unlike a newborn's skin, it is translucent and easily torn by the slightest pressure. Her thinning, white hair is sparse, exposing areas of pinkish-white scalp beneath.

Her mind is clear, a fact that adds to the emotional burden. She suffers most from the confinement of a failing body. The highlight of her day is the arrival of her daughter, Grace, who faithfully visits every day after work. Grace, who often feels exhausted after working long hours, makes every effort to visit her mother. She knows that her visits are pivotal to her mother's day.

As she walks down the long, familiar corridor, toward her mother's room, she can't help but think about the irony of their reversed roles. When Grace was a young schoolgirl she would come home for lunch; after school, she would return home and promptly begin her homework. Angeles, being a devoted, loving and committed working mother, telephoned Grace every day after school to ask, "How was your day dear? What did you have for lunch?"

And now it's Grace's turn. She stops at the desk to ask the nurses about her mother. "How was her day? What did she have for lunch?"

As she walks into her mother's room she is greeted by a tender smile and a warm glow. This sight would melt even the most hardened of hearts and rejuvenates Grace's tired, aching body.

On this particular day, Grace is not in the best of health. Her upset stomach kept her from sleeping most of the night. Angeles, with her insightful instinct, senses immediately that her daughter isn't well. "Not feeling well today?"

She denies feeling ill to spare her mother any worry, but Angeles insists something is wrong, and persists. "You never could fool me, Grace. I know you aren't yourself today. Please tell me what's wrong."

Grace gratefully slips into the soft chair next to her mother's wheelchair. "You are right, Mami. I'm not feeling well today. I remember how you took care of me when I was little and not feeling well. How you nursed me back to health with hot soup, tea and lots of tender, loving care. I remember how you used to lay beside me, caressing me gently, so I wouldn't feel lonely. You used to freshen my feverish face with a cool, dampened towel."

Turning to look directly into her mother's eyes she continues, "There were even times, Mami, when I didn't want to get well. Yes, that's right, so you would have to stay home with me longer and not go back to work. I remember those moments dearly, Mami. Now I'm a grown woman. I must tend to my own well-being. Who's going to take care of me now when I get sick?"

Her frail, devoted mother whispered, "I will, Grace. I will."

by Grace G. Martin

Grace G. Martin, MS, RD, is a nutrition educator and consultant. She gives presentations on basic and therapeutic nutrition during the life cycle. She can be reached at G. G. Martin Associates, 17 Covered Bridge Road, Neshanic Station, NJ 08853; Telephone: (908) 369-5446; Fax: (908) 369-5672; e-mail: ggmartin@worldnet.att.net.

A Love Note for Lilly

We cannot do great things . . . only small things with great love.
~ Mother Teresa

Lea glanced at the clock on the wall of the nurse's station. *One hour to go until the next shift comes in.* Lea could then devote her time to paperwork on her three new clients that had been settled in to quiet rooms with an aide. Lea was the only registered nurse on the ten-bed intensive care unit. She could always count on the community mental health center to provide challenges on the four to midnight shift. With the help of two mental health aides, things were under control for now. Lea started the paperwork on her new admission.

Just as she started a second chart, a police car pulled up to the entrance. *Oh, no!* she thought with mixed emotions. *Why do they always have to come in on my shift?* The officers dragged in a disheveled, belligerent young woman, who was restrained in hand cuffs that were attached to a waste chain and leg irons. They escorted her to a chair and positioned themselves on either side.

"I'm Lea, your nurse. What's your name?" Lea had never seen such a pathetic person. Her hardened face was drawn and she sneered at Lea with lifeless blue eyes.

"Go to hell!" The patient's response came, just as she lunged at Lea. The officers restrained her as she continued to scream a barrage of vulgarities.

Lea whispered softly, "Please tell me your name so I can help you."

The patient began to calm down as she answered, "Lilly. I don't want to talk right now. The cops can tell you whatever you want to know."

Lea asked the aide and one of the officers to take Lilly to the shower room and get her started on the admission procedure. The other officer followed Lea into the nurse's station.

"You really have your hands full with that one," he began. "We got the call about nine o'clock. She was shredding her apartment. When we arrived, she had overturned furniture, spread feces on the walls, torn the curtains from the windows and was throwing things. We had to transport her in cuffs and leg irons to control her. It would help if your facility wasn't so far away, but it's the closest mental facility that would care for the likes of her."

Lilly could be heard ranting and raving above the sound of the shower. Lea went to check on her while the policeman stood outside the door. The female aide was getting soaked in her attempt to help Lilly get shampooed. Lea poked her head around the shower curtain and asked, "Lilly, are you finished yet?"

"Give me a towel and let me get some clothes on. I'm not used to taking a shower with someone else in the room. I live alone!" At least she answered without obscenities this time.

Lea handed Lilly a towel as she said, "After you get dressed, maybe you'll tell me what's going on with you." The tirade started again and any effort to quiet Lilly only fueled the explosive behavior.

Lea whispered, "Lilly, I need to know if you are taking any medicines or if you have any allergies. I'm going to call the doctor so he can prescribe something that will help you regain control." The whispering seemed to quiet Lilly down.

"I used to take Haldol a long time ago. I can't always get to a doctor."

While the aide helped Lilly to finish dressing, Lea called the doctor and obtained an order for a Haldol injection and restraints as needed. Lilly's reaction was, "No way are you going to give me a shot . . . and you're not going to strap me down!" She was cursing at full volume. "I hope I wake up all the patients, then you'll have someone else to pick on!"

Earlier in her shift, Lea called her husband, telling him what a hectic evening it had been, adding, "Please say a prayer for me."

Lea silently prayed as she and the officers placed Lilly in restraints. After Lea gave the injection, she sat at Lilly's bedside, holding her hand and whispering words of encouragement. "The doctor will be here soon, and then I will be going home."

"Just go then. You're like all the rest. No one cares. No one loves me. Go on. Get out!" Lilly shouted.

"You're wrong, Lilly. I do love and care for you. Try and close your eyes now. You need some sleep. I'll stay a while and check on you before I go."

"Ya, so you say. How will I know that if I go to sleep you'll ever look at me again?"

Lea quickly thought of a solution. "Tell you what I'll do. I'll leave a note tucked under your pillow before I leave. Now close your eyes and try to sleep. Sh . . ." Lea continued to hold her hand until the medicine took affect. Lilly obediently closed her eyes and fell asleep.

It was now 11:30 p.m. Lea had two more charts to complete. With barely enough time to make a hurried call to her husband, Lea said, "Honey, it's going to be another late night. You go on to bed." She no sooner concluded her call when the doctor came in, examined Lilly, signed orders and immediately left.

Lea gave report and secluded herself in a conference room to finish charts. Then she wrote her note to Lilly, on a little yellow sticky note, which read, "Lilly, I love you." She signed it "Lea" and placed it under her pillow as promised.

The next day, Lilly was waiting for Lea to come in. She grabbed Lea's hand, held up the note and, smiling from ear to ear, said, "I really didn't think you'd remember. Thank you."

For the next three days Lilly was an exemplary patient, taking advantage of all the programs. Lea made time to talk with Lilly each day and encouraged her to talk about herself, offering her the hope of leading a productive life. On the fourth day Lea discovered that Lilly had indeed made progress. She had been transferred.

Almost a year went by until a familiar scenario was repeated. The police brought Lilly in again. Lilly started searching through her pockets when she saw Lea, pulling out a ragged piece of yellow paper held together with tape. Thrusting it toward Lea, she smiled.

"See, I still have the note you wrote me. I keep it with me all the time. That way I know someone still loves me."

As tears filled her eyes, Lea took the hapless figure into her arms, and they both cried. Lea never realized just how much a little love note could mean.

by joy lee

joy lee, an Oklahoma native, worked as a secretary and bookkeeper while raising her four children. Suddenly alone, after thirty years of marriage, she graduated as a registered nurse from Cameron University at age fifty-two. She worked at Jim Talliaferro Community Mental Health Center and Comanche County Health Department as Public Health Nurse. "This is the height of nursing, calling forth every ounce of strength and endurance."

Your Son Is Here

It is one of the most beautiful compensations of life, that no man can sincerely try to help another without helping himself.

~ Ralph Waldo Emerson

A few years back I had been out of town for ten days on a special assignment. Things were going well during my field visit in Florida when I heard the disturbing news. The area manager, who was also my boss, called to tell me that my father had a severe heart attack. Since there was some uncertainty as to whether my dad would even live through the day, he suggested that I head back to Chicago after I finished my morning business.

When I arrived at O'Hare airport, I called the hospital right away. They told me that my father's condition had improved slightly. They were able to stabilize him and move him to the coronary care unit. They assured me that, although he was still in critical condition, he was doing as well as could be expected. I felt somewhat better after that phone call.

Quickly, I hailed a taxi and went straight to the hospital to be with Dad. It was a comfort to know he was stable. When I finally arrived, the nurse told me that my father was having some testing done but it would only take about an hour. She showed me where I could comfortably wait for him in the visitor's lounge, just outside the coronary care unit.

I dozed off for a few minutes and awakened when I heard someone ask, "Richard, would you like to see your father now? Please come with me. I'll take you to him." I followed the nurse who escorted me to the bedside of an elderly man that I couldn't recognize.

"Your son is here to see you," she whispered softly to the pale man who was attached to an assortment of tubes and noisy devices. The old man didn't respond. "Your son is here," she said with more volume. She had to repeat the words several more times before the groggy man opened his eyes. With a contorted face, he tried to make his eyes focus on me. It appeared that he could barely see me, if at all.

"Son . . . " he whispered as he reached his hand out to me. I wrapped my fingers tightly around his trembling hand, squeezing a message of care and encouragement. The nurse brought me a chair and I sat for several hours at his side, holding the old man's hand and occasionally offering some gentle words of hope and love. The dying man closed his eyes and said nothing as he clung tightly to my hand.

As evening approached, he let go. The old man had died. I placed his lifeless hand on the bed and went to notify the nurse. I went back and stayed with him for a few minutes more.

The nurse came to offer me words of sympathy. I stopped her and said, "I didn't really know this man."

"But I thought he was your father?" the startled nurse responded. "Why didn't you say something when I took you to see him?"

"Because I knew he needed his son. His son just wasn't here at the time. When I realized he was too sick to tell whether I was his son or not, I knew how much he needed me. I felt the urgency to be here for him, so I stayed. I knew it was important to him. It was the right thing to do." Then I quietly left the room and went to the desk to ask for directions to my father's room.

by Richard Bourbeau

Richard Bourbeau is a man who enjoys sharing his life through writing. He believes that one life can make a difference. He can be reached at K 75708, Box 112, Joliet, IL. 60434-0112.

The Gift of Love

Remember the day, not so long ago, that unfamiliar voice,
which sweetly whispered in your ear, and then you made your
choice?

With the realization of that moment, you took the step to start,
you lit the fire of the lamp in hand, and the one inside your heart.

With that fire burning earnestly, you donned your wings and flew,
soaring ever gracefully, as if you always knew.

From deep inside, you drew your strength, your courage from
above,
to care for them with gentle hands, compassion, and with love.

A loving touch, a knowing look, to wipe away a tear,
Made all the difference between comfort, trust and fear.

And with each smile and grateful touch from those for whom you
cared, your heart was warmed and thankful for the moments that
you shared.

Remember the gifts of love you gave and those returned to you,
will keep the fire burning in everything you do.

You are a nurse, a caring person, touching many lives,
Keep this in mind, for you may be, someone's angel in disguise.

by Debra L. Skelly

Debra L. Skelly, RN, BSN, CPN, has been a registered nurse for nineteen years. After graduating from Seton Hall University, where she earned a BSN degree, she became a nationally Certified Pediatric Nurse. She enjoys her work on a Pediatric Unit at Monmouth Medical Center in Long Branch, New Jersey. She can be reached at 8 Wealthy Avenue, Middletown, NJ 07748; Telephone: (732) 495-5433; e-mail: Hera8301@aol.com.

Their Love Shined Through

*To love others is to realize their uniqueness and limitless possi-
bilities in the same way we value ours. When we say we love
someone we mean that we want them to be who they are and
not who we may want them to be just for our own convenience.*
                                            ~ Dr. Leo Buscaglia

Even though my parents were married for well over fifty years, I
still felt that they stayed together "for the sake of the children." In
this case, I was the *only child* and fifty-ish at that!

My parents were both active and healthy, well into their
eighties. At eighty-five years old, Dad suffered a stroke. While he
was recovering in the hospital, I saw my parents' love shine through
like never before. I watched Dad reach his hand out for Mom to
hold. I noticed as he firmly pulled her toward him for a kiss on the
lips. In my lifetime I had never witnessed these outward signs of
love by my parents.

Mom, a registered nurse from yesteryear, still had the magic
touch of an "angel of mercy." Within six months, she had Dad
walking with a cane and back to taking the bus to the Senior Center
to play cards and dance! Of course, Dad didn't play cards or dance
quite the same as before, but he still gave it all he had.

Gradually, Dad's health failed and soon after his eighty-eighth
birthday he was hospitalized. During the next four months, he
spent only a few days at home, in between visits to the hospital
and nursing homes. The doctors never found out exactly what the
problem was, but we knew. His time here with us was running
out.

Mom would visit Dad faithfully every day, and sometimes
even twice a day. Of course, being from the old school, she made
sure he had the cleanest laundry and the tastiest treats. While I
was at work, Mom took the bus to the hospital to see him in the
afternoon. She made certain the doctors, nurses and staff gave him

the finest care. Each day he would reach out to hold Mom's hand and kiss her lips.

Dad was again admitted to the hospital one month before their sixtieth wedding anniversary. His health continued to fail, and we all knew his time with us would soon be over, even before the doctors told us.

Two days before their wedding anniversary, I took the rare opportunity to have a private visit with Dad, on my way home from work. He wasn't conscious, but he held my hand firmly. We had the best talk of our lives, although I did all the talking. I reminded him that his sixtieth wedding anniversary was the next day, and assured him that it was okay with us if he wanted to miss this one. I thanked him for everything he had done for me as my dad. I also asked him to forgive me for my short comings, as I forgave him his.

The salty tears rolled freely down my face as I spoke. Finally I said, "I know that we both did our best, Dad." Then I just sat quietly in the chair for a few moments, watching him "sleep." As I prepared to leave, I took his thin, frail hand in mine and whispered, "I love you, Dad." His trembling hand responded in acknowledgment.

The next day, Mom and I brought anniversary cards and flowers to share with Dad. That evening Mom and I went out for a simple, but special anniversary dinner with my wife. The three of us sat at a table for four—the fourth place symbolizing Dad's loving presence.

When Mom and I arrived at the hospital the following afternoon, Dad's nurse stopped us in the hallway. He stood quietly in front of the door and reached out his hand, placing it on my shoulder. There was no need for words. We knew Dad was gone. Mom held Dad's hand and gave him one last kiss, as their love shined through.

by Tom Lagana

Tom Lagana is a professional speaker, author and professional engineer. With more than thirty years' experience, Tom has worked with corporate clients throughout the world. He is co-author of *Chicken Soup for the Prisoner's Soul* and *Chicken Soup for the Volunteer's Soul*, a member of the National Speakers Association and 1994 recipient of the Jefferson Award for Outstanding Public Service. He can be reached at Success Solutions, P.O. Box 7816, Wilmington, DE 19803; e-mail: Success@TomLagana.com; Web site: http://www.TomLagana.com.

Love and Compassion in Maximum Security

The supreme happiness in life is the conviction that we are loved.
~ Victor Hugo

My sixteen-year career in the field of substance abuse treatment has been one of many rewards. My work has provided me with the opportunity to see people's lives transformed, as they overcome their addictions, convert apathy into empathy and develop a sense of love and compassion for others.

I firmly believe that two of the greatest needs of this day are love and compassion for our fellowman. These two elements eliminate hate and prejudice that are vital to living in a world of peace and harmony.

In 1992, I was privileged to witness an act of unselfishness and a very profound demonstration of love and compassion. I share this experience in an effort to stem the tide of skepticism concerning the effectiveness of substance abuse treatment within a prison setting and to reinforce the notion that people can, and do, change. I also want to highlight the fact that love and compassion can still be found, even in a very hostile and negative environment as a maximum security prison.

In the summer of 1992, James, one of the residents participating in a prison-based substance abuse treatment program, was diagnosed with cancer of the lymph nodes. As his condition worsened, he was transferred from the treatment unit to the prison infirmary, to live his final days in seclusion and be provided with the necessary medical services.

I would go to the infirmary regularly to visit with James to provide support. He was reluctant to ask for anything specific, but was always appreciative of everything that was given to him. On many of these trips, I would deliver to him various items such as soft-drinks, coffee, chips and cookies donated by the residents that were participating in the treatment program.

At his request, James was periodically escorted from the infirmary to the treatment unit. He would usually stay about an hour visiting with his friends in the program. The residents would rally around him and make every attempt to cheer him up, some telling jokes, others giving him a poem or a drawing, a cup of coffee or just a genuine smile. As he would depart they would line up to give him a hug and offer words of encouragement. He always left the unit smiling and waving farewell. I often wondered, *Which visit would be his last? Which trip would he be waving a final farewell?*

As his condition worsened, he could not walk due to swelling in his feet and legs, but he still contended that he wanted to visit his friends in the program. Residents would volunteer to go to the infirmary to help him into a wheelchair and push him to and from the unit. His visits lessened and even though he was weaker and in more pain with each passing day, James managed to smile and lift his hand up high to wave farewell each time he departed the cell-block.

In late July, Darrell, a new graduate of the program, approached the program staff and made an unusual request. He stated that James had told him about his fear of dying alone in prison. Since James only had a short time to live, Darrell asked for permission to visit with him in the infirmary, so he could be there to make the inevitable less fearful for a dying man in prison.

With special permission granted from the Warden, Darrell was allowed to sit with James each day from 4:00 p.m. until 6:00 a.m. Although James was becoming weaker, and death was knocking on his door, Darrell was there for him on a daily basis, giving him hope and inspiring him not to give up his fight for life.

Darrell would spend his evenings and nights doing everything possible to make James more comfortable. Darrell would read to him, write letters and make phone calls for him. He bathed and shaved him, fed him when he felt like eating, wrapped his swollen feet with bandages and lifted him up when the nurse would come in to give him medicine.

In the later stages of his illness, James lost control over bladder and bowel functions. Darrell was always there to patiently clean him and change his bed clothes and sheets, trying to make each occurrence less humiliating for James. Darrell took special care of James, much like a loving father would take care of his dying son.

Despite all efforts by the medical staff at the prison, and Darrell's devotion to be there with his friend to make his last days on earth easier, James finally gave up his battle for life. He passed away in his assigned bed, in a maximum-security prison, on September 16, 1992.

On this day he gained his freedom—freedom from pain, suffering and incarceration. But thank God he died with dignity and left this world knowing he had one true friend, Darrell, who showered him with love and compassion. Yes, people can change, and love and compassion still exists, even in a maximum-security prison.

by Bob Kennington

Bob Kennington has worked in prison-based therapeutic communities for more than ten years. He can be reached at 10 Burton Hills Boulevard, Nashville, TN 37215; e-mail: BOBJAKE99@aol.com.

Reprinted by permission Bob Kennington. Copyright ©1993 Bob Kennington. (Based on a story previously published in *Chicken Soup for the Prisoner's Soul*, Jack Canfield, Mark Victor Hansen and Tom Lagana, pg 214, Health Communications, Inc., 3201 S.W. 15th St., Deerfield Beach, Florida, 33442-8190; Copyright ©2000.)

[*EDITOR'S NOTE*: For information contact the **National Prison Hospice Association,** P.O. Box 3769, Boulder, CO 80307-3769; Telephone: (303) 544-5923; Fax: (303) 444-2824; e-mail: npha@npha.org; Web site: http://www.npha.org.]

A Single Act of Love

The hunger for love is much more difficult to remove than the hunger for bread.

~ Mother Teresa

His brief but tormented young life was punctuated by recurring visits to hospital emergency rooms for treatment of unexplained, questionable injuries too numerous to count. He was a small boy who always had a smile for everyone. Only God knows what horrors he was made to endure at home.

The responsible adults who were supposed to be caring for him couldn't even control their own anger, impulses and frustrations. His family and friends, and the social system that was intended to protect him, failed him miserably. He shouldn't have been allowed to slip through the cracks; but somehow, in this imperfect world, he did.

On his last hospital admission, this battered and wounded young child received exceptional care, and perhaps some of the only loving and caring moments of comfort and safety he would ever know in his abbreviated life.

That evening, the nurse who was taking care of this broken four-year-old boy, climbed into his bed, lay down next to him and cuddled him close to her heart. She gently stroked his forehead and sang lullabies softly into his ear until he fell asleep. That night, he closed his tiny eyes for the last time. Those beautiful lullabies were hopefully the last sounds he would hear.

This little boy passed into the next life surrounded by the love that he so desperately needed and deserved in this one. A single act of love, performed by one special nurse, unafraid to use her mind as well as her heart, made a big difference to this precious little angel.

by Laura Lagana, RN

A Second Chance

Dost thou love life? Then do not squander time, for that's the stuff life is made of.

~ Benjamin Franklin

How many times have you said to yourself, *If only I could do it over again*, or *If only I had a second chance?* Most of us never get a second chance. Our lives are busy, time eludes us and death arrives before we're finished with our work here on earth. This wasn't true in John's case.

I was a young, ambitious head nurse in charge of the coronary care unit (CCU) where John arrived eighteen years ago. He was a sixty-year-old general contractor who was used to being in charge and who immediately took charge over me. He had been admitted to our hospital with crushing chest pain unrelieved by intravenous narcotics; diagnosis–Acute Myocardial Infarction (heart attack).

John was anxious and feeling his loss of control. He hollered and ordered the nurses around. He shouted, "Get my doctor over here immediately!" Suddenly, his sinus rhythm converted to ventricular tachycardia, then to fibrillation, a commonplace occurrence in a CCU. Call a code . . . remember the ABCs of CPR and defibrillate . . . a quick, successful code. This man was now back to ordering us around.

John urgently wanted to see his family, especially his young granddaughter, Carlie. He directed me to call them at once. This was his second chance at life, but little did I know my life was about to be changed forever.

In those days, cardiac care centered on "resting the heart" so it could build collateral circulation. Activity was limited to minimize cardiac output, which meant bedrest and liquid diets. Personal hygiene had to be done exclusively by the nurse. John resisted, complained and tried to reinvent the system. He watched the nurses, much like a contractor would watch over his workers. He knew who did their job, who did it well and who he would fire in a minute. ₹

John made the nurses feel uncomfortable so I usually assigned myself to his care. In nursing school I learned to be a professional. I was taught never to get personally involved with my patients, but that wasn't part of John's plan. He viewed people as he must have viewed his blueprints over the years–he looked at them from an architect's vantage point, observing their many facets, imperfections and beauty.

With the perception of an engineer, John would look for strengths and weaknesses to determine where changes or additions could be made. In a spiritual sense, he believed that I was responsible for his new lease on life. It was clear that John was indebted to me and he enjoyed his role as my newly assigned guardian angel. He wanted to help shape my life.

After his discharge from the hospital, he would stop by to say hello or bring a box of candy for the nurses. John was elated when I announced I was expecting my first child. He would greet me in the parking lot after work with fresh fruits and vegetables to ensure my child's good health, as if he were an expectant grandfather.

After the birth of my daughter, Meghan, he visited us at the hospital. His love for children brought him even closer to our lives. John would sporadically check-in with short, five-minute phone calls, just to tell me he was okay and to see if things were going well with me. He was there for the christening, remembered birthdays and Christmases, and even left Easter baskets on our doorstep. My daughter thought he was mystical, like Santa Claus. My husband and I were wined and dined like royalty at his daughter's wedding.

Years passed and my three additional daughters had grown to love John as a grandpa. His visits became fewer and shorter as his cardiac disease, diabetes and kidney failure, with three-days-a-week of dialysis, limited him physically. But he was still in charge. He would fire his doctors and call the health department to report adverse conditions at the dialysis center.

John even passed his drivers test when a family member reported him to the Division of Motor Vehicles. He wore his Marine Corp hat to the test as a symbol of his competency. His family couldn't clip his wings, and he was proud of the fact that he could still outwit them.

John's second chance allowed him to see five new grandchildren of his own, the heartache of a son's divorce and the untimely death of a grandson he so desperately wanted to help. John was there to watch young Carlie grow into a young lady and go off to college; and to see Eric, his grandson, play in the Little League World Series. I almost felt as if I were related to his family when he shared his stories with us.

John's last visit was special. He saw all four of my daughters and pointed out what made each uniquely special. Several times during this visit he looked straight at me and asked, "How are you doing, June?" He needed to know that I was happy and would be all right. I felt truly loved.

A few days later John called to say he couldn't visit anymore. He was back in the hospital with a heart rate over 170 beats per minute.

He laughed when I said, "John, after twenty years of marriage, I never even had that effect on my own husband." I could just picture his smile as he chuckled over the phone. John certainly was a charmer.

One week later, resuscitation was unsuccessful and John's second chance ran out. His daughter called us with the news. She knew her father had a special place in our hearts. I felt connected to his family at the funeral. We had all shared in John's love.

Although my heart is still heavy, I know an angel has been assigned to watch over me.

by June Curti

June Curti, RN, BSN, is currently a school nurse and has her own public speaking and personal coaching business. She has been a nurse since 1975. She can be reached at 80 Post Circle, Clark, NJ 07066; Telephone: (732) 388-6311; Fax: (732) 388-5357; e-mail: BeYou1234@aol.com.

[*EDITOR'S NOTE*: For information contact the **American Heart Association**, 7272 Greenville Avenue, Dallas, TX 75231-4596; Telephone: (800) 242-8721 (Voice: Toll-free); (214) 706-1552 (Voice); Fax: (214) 706-2139; e-mail: inquire@amhrt.org; Web site: http://www.americanheart.org.]

CHAPTER 2
PEARLS OF WISDOM

True wisdom lies in gathering the precious things out of each day as it goes by.

~ E. S. Bouton

Why Do These Things Have to Happen?

One of my joys and passions is to sing. I love to perform in our local theaters. My throat got very sore during preparation for a particularly grueling show. It was my first time to try an operatic piece. I was terrified that I had actually done damage to my vocal cords. I had a lead part and the show was about to open.

I made an appointment and took off work to see our family doctor, where I waited . . . and waited . . . for sixty minutes. I finally left in a huff, went back to work, grabbed a phone book and found a throat specialist close by. Once more I made an appointment for that afternoon. Off I went.

The nurse showed me in, and I sat down to wait for the doctor. I felt disgruntled. I rarely get sick, and here I was sick when I needed to be healthy and sing. Besides, I had to take time out of my work day to go to two different doctors, both of whom kept me waiting. Frustrating! *Why do these things have to happen?*

A moment later the nurse came back in and asked, "May I ask you something personal?" This seemed odd. *What else do they ask you but personal questions in a doctor's office?* "I noticed your hand," she continued.

I had lost most of my left hand in a forklift accident when I was eleven. I think it is one of the reasons I didn't follow my dream of performing in theater, although everyone says, "I never noticed. You are so natural." In the back of my mind was the thought, *They only want to see perfect people up there. Besides, I'm too tall, overweight and not really talented. No, they don't want to see me.*

But I love musical comedies, and they tell me I have a good voice. So one day I tried out at our local community theater. I was the first one they cast. Since then I have been cast in many roles and recently played the lead in "Hello, Dolly!"

I looked at the nurse and replied, "Yes, of course."

She seemed hesitant, then repeated, "I noticed your hand. What I need to know is, how has it affected your life?"

Never in the years since it happened has anyone asked me this. They say, "Does it bother you?" But never anything this sweeping.

After an awkward pause, she continued, "You see, I just had a baby, and her hand is like yours. I . . . well . . . I need to know how it has affected your life."

How has it affected your life? I thought about it a bit before I could crystallize what was right to reply. Then these words came out:

Losing my hand has affected my life, but not in a bad way. I do many things people with two normal hands find difficult. I touch-type seventy-five words a minute with one hand and play the lute. I also ride and have shown horses in horse shows and have earned a Horsemaster Degree. I'm involved in musical theater, am a professional speaker and work with my mom, Dottie Walters, booking speakers in Walters Speakers Bureau. I do television shows four or five times a year.

It was never "difficult" for me because of my family. They always talked about all the great notoriety I would get because I would learn how to do things with one hand most people had trouble doing with two. What I could do was the main focus, not the handicap.

I explained to the troubled nurse, "Your daughter does not have a problem. She is normal. You are the one that will teach her to think of herself as anything else. She will come to know she is *different*, but you will teach her different is wonderful. Normal means you are average. What's fun about that?"

The nurse was silent for awhile, then she simply said, "Thank you," and walked out. I sat there thinking, *Everything happens for a reason, even that forklift crushing my hand—all the circumstances leading up to my being at this doctor's office, at this moment in time, and being here when the nurse needed me.* Then the doctor came in. After he looked at my throat, he said he wanted to anesthetize it and insert a probe in order to examine it.

Singers are paranoid about putting medical instruments down their throats, especially ones so rough you need to be anesthetized. I said, "No thanks," and walked out.

Next day? My throat was totally well. Why do these things happen?

by Lillet Walters

Lillet Walters is a best selling author about speakers, and an executive at Walters Speakers Bureau. She can be reached at P.O. Box 398, Glendora, CA 91740; (626) 335-8069; Web site: http://www.aboutonehandtyping.com.

Your Best Shot

The world is filled with beauty, joy and wonder, along with ugliness, hatred and violence. In my youth, I always believed that things were either black or white; people were either good or bad; that is, until I grew up.

When I became a nurse I saw many different sides of life, witnessed things that defied explanation and learned life isn't always fair. As I became a wife and mother, I discovered the gray zone that lies between the black and the white. I also discovered that there are no guarantees in life. You give it your best shot and hope that it's good enough. With this same attitude my husband and I approached parenthood. We both agreed that we would do our best to raise our two sons to be honest, law-abiding citizens.

I viewed both parenthood and my part-time position as medical-surgical nurse at one of our local hospitals as a journey into the unknown. Parenthood and nursing always yielded unexpected challenges and sometimes hidden rewards. I faced fear many times during my nursing career.

One December morning, I was "pulled" to the Protective Care Unit (PCU). When there was a staffing shortage in the hospital, the nurses would be "pulled" to that particular department that was in need. For some reason, I feared the PCU. I knew the unit was used to isolate patients suffering from infectious diseases, for reverse isolation to protect patients with compromised immune systems and to house inmates from the local prison who needed treatment.

For whatever reason, my fear remained strong. After morning report, the change-of-shift meeting where patient assignments and updates are given, I prepared to care for my assigned patients. Suddenly I was forced to face my worst fear.

I was assigned to take care of a prison inmate—a convict. Suddenly I stopped breathing. I could hardly swallow let alone speak, so I began to review my patients' charts. I reviewed the inmate's chart last, foolishly trying to postpone the inevitable. I decided to conceal my fear and meet my patients.

When I met the prisoner, he wasn't at all what I expected. In my mind's eye I expected to see a large, disheveled, abusive character—instead, I saw a frightened, sickly child who desperately needed help. Jamie had appendicitis and was shackled to the bed, which was customary procedure for inmates. A correctional officer was posted at his bedside around the clock.

Jamie was amazingly frail and only several years older than our own two teenage sons. He tried to find a more comfortable position, despite the shackles. After I introduced myself and pulled up a chair, I began to explain his upcoming surgery to him. I quickly lost my fear, and I was determined to help alleviate his fears by preparing him for the operation.

Despite his obvious pain and discomfort, Jamie was eager to talk to me. As I took his vital signs and began washing his scarred face, he said with a grimace, "You know, you remind me so much of my mother. You could be her sister. You're so much like my dear, sweet mother. We had such good times. This time of year we'd bring in that huge Christmas tree, and then decorate it. Dad made sure to put that star on the top. Then we'd bake all kinds of cookies with icing and candies. Then, on Christmas morning, there'd be hundreds of presents under the tree and a big fire blazing in the stone fireplace. Oh, those were the good old days," he said. When the vomiting returned, Jamie had to stop for a few minutes. After I cleaned him up, he continued to reminisce. "I sure miss those days. And I really miss my six brothers and sisters—three of each you know."

"I'll bet you do miss those good times. At least you have wonderful memories," I replied. I didn't know what else to say. I couldn't stop wondering. *How does such a nice young man go so wrong? Just what happens to a person?* I never asked, because I didn't want to know—and I didn't need to know.

I read Jamie's chart and made a few notes. As I looked over his history and admission notes, I couldn't believe my eyes. Jamie had been abandoned at birth and had never known a mother or father.

He spent his entire twenty-two years going in and out of foster homes and juvenile detention facilities—never knowing his natural parents—never knowing unconditional love.

This time, Jamie was serving real time in prison. I knew he had to have done something serious. I'm glad I didn't know what it was. I didn't want to think in terms of black or white, good or bad. I prayed that I could be a good enough mother to my sons so this wouldn't happen to them—but there are no guarantees.

The time for surgery approached. The orderly pushed the gurney and accompanied me to Jamie's room. When the gurney and bed were aligned and the officer released Jamie's shackles, we helped him onto the gurney. As I pulled the sheet over him and placed the green paper cap on his head, Jamie looked at me through glassy eyes, a sign that the preoperative medication had taken effect. I felt the urgency to say something, so I took his hand in mine and said, "When you are released from prison, don't ever go back—make sure you stay out. Will you do that for me?"

He squeezed my hand and with a dry-mouthed, raspy voice responded, "Thanks, Mom . . . Thanks. I'll do my best."

I don't know if I made much of a difference that day, but I'd like to think so. Jamie, if you are reading this story, I pray to God that you are reading this from the "outside." I hope you gave it your best shot.

by Laura Lagana, RN

Reprinted by permission of Laura Lagana, RN. Copyright ©1999 Laura Lagana, RN. (Previously published in *Chicken Soup for the Prisoner's Soul*, Jack Canfield, Mark Victor Hansen and Tom Lagana, pg 203, Health Communications, Inc., 3201 S.W. 15th St., Deerfield Beach, Florida, 33442-8190; Copyright ©2000.)

[*EDITOR'S NOTE*: For information on how to purchase *Chicken Soup for the Prisoner's Soul*, which is NOT available in bookstores, write to Prisoner's Soul, P.O. Box 7816, Wilmington, DE 19803, or see Web site: http://www.TomLagana.com.]

THE DEEP END by Matt Matteo

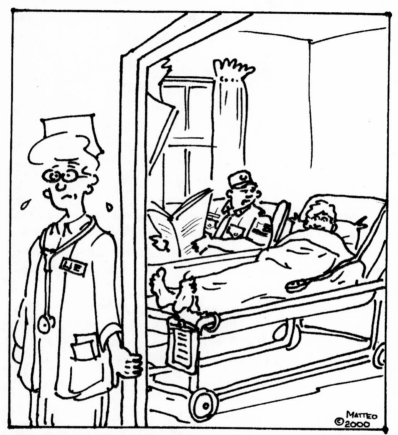

GRIPPED WITH FEAR, NURSE Jo PREPARED
HERSELF BEFORE TREATING HER FIRST
INMATE.

Reprinted by permission of Matt Matteo.

The Color White

Before you read on, you must fathom my aversion to the color of white. My mother was a nurse who died of cancer when I was three years old. I was born with a plethora of congenital bone deformities. I felt as if I were a box of broken toys they were forever patching and replacing.

As a child, I knew the orthopedic ward as well as my own room. Legend has it that I was so overwrought whenever I saw a nurse's uniform that my mother had to change her clothes when she came home from work, before she picked me up and lifted me out of my crib. To me, white meant needles and casts and agony; it was not the color of cleanliness, purity, angel lace or baby powder lightly spilled upon a rug.

It was a summer day and very hot. I remember the sheets, their starched and waiting envelopes, the pillows of stone, walls without pictures, curtains rolling back and forth, but I cannot recall my age, when one nurse in a little white hat left her mark upon my soul.

When I awoke in terrible pain after surgery, they gave me shot after shot after shot, until they ran out of "flesh space," as Nettie put it. I knew I had to eat. In front of me was a small bowl of gelatin. I was hungry and nauseated at the same time, so I let her put the spoon to my mouth.

The bowl was half-pink and half-green: cherry and mint. I ate the cherry gelatin, but refused the mint, throwing a typical child's fit and frenzy, when my father, a doctor, walked into the room. He ordered me to behave, to apologize and to eat—all of which I did obediently. When I swallowed the green gunk, I promptly barfed all over the nurse and was terribly troubled by the mess I had made. I'd lived my life like an itching pony in the stable of my father's approval barn, never wanting to fan a spark of disappointment into a fire. He seemed so perfect that I didn't dare to be less.

I was expecting some punishment, but Nettie just laughed and said, "Even when you make a mess, you do it in rainbows. But this is just a little more color than I'd planned for this day, child." I looked at her, floating on a passing thought. *So this is what my mom was like.* It was as if a piece of my mother had fallen from the sky and someone picked her up, placing her on my bed.

Hours later, or so it seemed, when all was quiet and the mess was erased like a dusty chalkboard at school, Nettie reappeared with a big fat chocolate bar in her hand. "This is for you, but don't you tell, or we're both goin' home by the seat of our pants!" I promised quietude and said my prayers out loud that night.

Years passed and I adjusted well to my amputation. When I was nineteen, the bones in my unformed hip slipped together and were pinching the sciatic nerve. They had to do a dangerous, experimental operation in an effort to salvage what motion I still had. The doctors feared they would split my femur, which was half the normal size, in two when they drove the steel rod down its center. To keep my busy body still, they pinned me in a huge body cast.

When I came to, a dozen wilted roses lay in a vase beside my bed. The drugs kept me under the covers of fitful sleep for an entire week. I was mad! They were reinserting a catheter into my urinary tract and the bubble of agony burst, like a comet colliding with earth. My skin felt like sweaty pantyhose I wanted to remove, only I couldn't.

I started to cry and said some irascible things to the young nurse who was fumbling with the tubes. In an instant, Nettie's face appeared. Her hair was gray now, washed by the tarnish of time and strife that every good nurse wears. She politely dismissed the younger nurse and calmed me down. "You grew up, sweetheart," she said, "but you haven't changed one bit. Still a little stinker, I see." We both laughed and the catheter went in less painfully.

The body cast was a veritable prison and my skin itched terribly. Nettie went to the closet and took out a small electric fan, positioning it to blow on just the right spots. I started to smile and my mind returned. "I hear you're in college now and writing poetry. May I read some?" she asked.

I steered her fingers to a plastic notebook in the night-stand drawer, then fell asleep, under the blanket of a breeze. When I awoke, she was sitting in the darkened room, her eyes awash with tears.

After she left, I flipped through the notebook and saw her fingerprints, mostly on my pages of my pain. She hadn't read the flippant stuff, that I thought was so clever, as carefully. I scribbled a line in my head, *White has deeper color than artists have given it credit for.*

When it came time for my release, Nettie helped me bundle up my things and wheeled me out the door. She gave me a hug, and I pressed a penciled poem into her hand. I think both our hips were hurting from the reach.

A silver tress dropped down from her nurse's cap and touched my cheek. My fingers put it back in place, like the rocking marigold shifting in sand beside my mother's grave.

by Janet I. Buck

Janet I. Buck's poetry, essays and fiction have appeared in hundreds of print and internet journals world-wide. She has four books on the market: *Calamity's Quilt, Reefs we Live, Bookmarks in a Hurricane, and Desideratum's Doggie Dish*, all of which are available at: http://www.janetbuck.com. She can be reached at 1642 Hollyhock Drive, Medford, OR 97504; Telephone: (541) 608-6595; e-mail: JBuck22874@aol.com.

Breaking down the Walls   .

Gifts make their way through stone walls.

~ Proverb

My neighbor died last night, somewhere in Peru. Doris had returned to the town of her birth to be with her family during her final days. A brain tumor had crept up on her silently, taking her vitality in what seemed like an instant, leaving behind sadness and emptiness.

Our friendship, though not close, always had a neighborly quality. She gave me lemon mint to plant in my yard and offered pleasant greetings whenever we met. That is, until Christmas morning, 1993.

I awoke to a startling, thundering crash. Either lightening had struck, or Santa Claus had taken a wrong turn. I leaped out of bed and dashed from room to room, looking for the cause, when what to my wondering eyes should appear in the back bedroom but daylight and a front fender.

One peek out the window revealed Doris, dazed and struggling out of her car. Fortunately, she aimed just right. A few inches less and she would have sent a large, glass-framed picture crashing down on my sleeping head. A few inches further and she would have hit the gas meter. She was stunned. Her actions were inexplicable, most of all to herself.

Once I determined she was unharmed, and the car had been pulled out of the house and towed away, I started the painful process of assessing the damages to both my house and psyche.

What Doris didn't know was that I sat up most of that night thinking about my relationship with my boyfriend, Michael. We determined that there was really no point in continuing on together. We thought it would be better to end it before too much more was at stake so we decided to spend a brief Christmas together and then go our separate ways.

Things didn't turn out that way though. As the seams of my house were ripped open that Christmas morning, so were the seams of my heart. The breach in my walls felt like an opening in my soul. Up until then, I tended to my emotional self-protection as I tended to my house; both provided me with refuge, solace and isolation. Except to my patients, I wasn't often willing to reveal my vulnerability.

Now, as my house stood exposed to the December cold, my heart felt vulnerable to the world. The protective shell had been cracked and the elements were rushing in. Michael stayed with me that Christmas day. He witnessed it all—the nurse calm under pressure and the woman wrenched by emotion. He saw a tender side of me that I hadn't been willing to share with him before. I suspect that he liked what he saw because we were married in the spring. I can't imagine how our lives would have turned out had we really said goodbye.

To offer her comfort, I went to see Doris before she left for Peru. After all, oncology was my specialty. She told me of her plans, and we cried together. Like so many times before, she questioned what "bad things" she might have done to deserve such a fate. Her husband said, "Maybe God was punishing you for driving your car into that house." I knew instantly that they still felt ashamed. I assured them that the accident was ancient history to me.

"Doris, you're responsible for saving the best thing in my life," I said. "Broken walls can be plastered but hearts are meant to be open." We both laughed at the irony. I left her with a promise to come with a supply of tissues next time.

We met a few more times before Doris left for Peru. Her husband spoke with me a week before she died. A neighbor told me just how much my visits had meant to Doris. My words brought her peace so that she could finally let go of her shame.

Imagine what I would have missed if: I hadn't spoken to her when I did; or if I hadn't visited her during her difficult times; or if I hadn't spoken from my heart, but rather from that place of self-protection. I can't imagine how my life would have turned out if Doris hadn't torn down the walls that Christmas morning.

by Nancy Harris Anderson

Nancy Harris Anderson, RN, BSN, OCN, has practiced nursing in a variety of specialties: geriatric medical/surgical, stroke rehab, renal dialysis and oncology. She is now a case manager in the Utilization Management Department of Alliance, PPO, a subsidiary of Mid Atlantic Medical Services, Inc. Nancy is married and also enjoys gardening, writing and meditation. She can be reached at 13309 Banbury Place, Silver Spring, MD 20904; Telephone: (301) 879-5699.

What We Learn about Ourselves

As a registered nurse, studying for a graduate degree in nursing, I decided to do an internship at a hospice. After all, I knew that I wasn't afraid of death. My work with one specific patient, Martha, made me realize just how dishonest I was with myself.

I immediately learned that my desire to elude death was almost as strong as my desire to help her. It was an exercise in powerful self-discipline just to remain with her as she journeyed toward death.

Despite my feelings of severe anxiety, those first few meetings with Martha were delightful. She was very intelligent, and took great joy in entertaining me with her sharp wit. As we spent time together, she became increasingly more comfortable with me—so comfortable that she began to confide in me.

"I just want to die. I'm not afraid of dying, not really," Martha would declare each day. "Death would be much better than . . . ," her voice hesitated momentarily as she finished with, "than living this way."

Contrary to what she said, she looked frightened. She talked about her guilt in being a terrible mother and her disappointment in not accomplishing much in her lifetime. She met with her children, and they were loving towards her. She took antidepressants and talked about her fears but continued to be self-critical and fearful.

One day she cried out, "Let me go! Let me go!" When I asked where she wanted to go, she replied, "To my Redeemer!"

Martha eventually became weaker with intermittent episodes of psychotic behavior and unresponsiveness alternating with periods of clarity. She looked like a skeleton with skin stretched over her bones. Her mental torment was overwhelming. I wanted to run but I didn't. I could feel and taste her isolation, fear and helplessness. Her world was without color, love or connection. It was then that the inevitable realization occurred. *This could happen to me.*

It became increasingly more difficult to visit with Martha. One cold and dreary January day, I thought seriously about staying home rather than visiting her. Somehow I forced myself to go. I decided that now was the time to tell her what I had intended to say for a long time. I don't know whether she even heard me. She was too weak to respond.

I told Martha how I identified with her when she talked about her self-critical and judgmental feelings; how I learned that I was much more critical of myself than others were; and how important it is to love and accept ourselves as we are.

"I don't think you will ever have to suffer again, where you are going," I whispered. At that moment in time I lost my own anxiety. I felt connected to her and had a feeling of peace and purpose.

As I left her bedside I felt nourished. Martha's wish was granted that night.

by Dorothy J. Smith

Dorothy J. Smith, RN, has been a psychiatric nurse in a hospital setting for more than twenty-five years. She has earned her Bachelor's Degree in Allied Health Services, and her Master's Degree in Counseling. Dorothy is an active member of the Congregational Church, and enjoys bringing psychology and spirituality together to benefit others. She can be reached at Telephone: (860) 644-6482.

Rosa's Prophecy

*The best and most beautiful things in the world cannot be seen
or even touched, they must be felt with the heart.*

~ Helen Keller

Rosa was, by far, the most fascinating and mysterious patient that
I have ever encountered in my nursing career. She wore brilliantly
colored scarves in her long, wavy, bleached-blonde curls, despite
the scorn of her physicians and the head nurse.

At first, I was unsure of Rosa's mental stability. Her many
years on the road as a gypsy made her curious appearance easier to
accept, although her accessories clashed with the hospital's blue,
snowflake-adorned gown. Countless wrinkles in her weathered face
revealed a long, harsh life and her deep-set brown eyes seemed to
exude vast wisdom.

Rosa had been admitted for testing and pharmaceutical trials
to determine how to more effectively manage the tremors and other
symptoms caused by Parkinson's Disease that made her life so
distressing.

She took great pride in reading the palms of the staff members.
Being a skeptic, I thought palm reading was simply hocus-pocus
and immediately dismissed the idea as nonsense. I used every excuse
in the book to keep my palms from being scrutinized.

One day we were seriously short-staffed, and I was coaxed into
working a double shift. Unexpectedly, I had more time to care for
Rosa, and I quickly became fascinated with her conversations. She
reminisced about life as a gypsy, her many loves and hair-raising
adventures. Rosa also confided that she had no living relatives or
friends. I thought, *How sad she has to be alone in the autumn of her
years. It doesn't seem fair.*

Despite her circumstances, Rosa always remained optimistic.
That evening she insisted on reading my palms. Occupied with
treatments and medications yet to be administered, I promised

my palms for later, saying, "I'll be back later, if things quiet down." *Perhaps this was how Rosa coped with her loneliness,* I surmised.

Eventually the hectic pace slackened a bit. As I made final rounds, bringing medications, giving backrubs and tucking my patients in for the night, I finally came to Rosa's room.

I sat on her bed. She stared into my eyes and took my hands in hers, quietly contemplating the rambling lines in my rough, red palms. With trembling hands, she meticulously manipulated my palms in order to see every detail, examining every skin fold along her journey.

As Rosa began her prophecy, her mysterious words seemed strangely believable. My disbelief was quickly transformed into respect for her apparent clairvoyance. Rosa predicted that I would fall madly in love with someone I had met previously, and our courtship would be short but intense.

"Your life will be happy, your love unwavering and you will travel." Stopping briefly to take a closer look, Rosa furrowed her eyebrows and continued, "There will be children—boys. Your journeys will take you into the community, hands-on with the public, and you will be instrumental in helping people." Rosa lifted her wobbly head and looked into my eyes, adding, "God is using these hands for His purpose. Let Him lead you. Follow your heart and trust your love." With a serene smile she held my hands tenderly within hers, palms together, for a few moments. Before letting go, she gave them a shaky, delicate squeeze, thanking me for taking good care of her.

Her words were remarkably believable. She had a magnetism that held me spellbound. Maybe I simply *wanted* to believe her. I wasn't dating anyone at the time, and I didn't believe in palmistry until that evening.

I gave Rosa her medications and massaged her aching back. Her tired body wasn't responding as well as her doctors had expected, but the backrub seemed to relax her. She never complained. It was difficult to know how she really felt. I watched this mysterious and loving woman drift off to sleep before I left her room.

After enjoying two days off, and thinking about the

extraordinary palm-reading session, I reported for the day shift. The unexpected news that Rosa had died during my absence came as a shock. I never had the chance to thank the "gypsy" who so accurately predicted my future.

Many chapters have been added to my life since then, but Rosa's words still remain in my heart. Weeks later, fate did bring someone into my life; someone I had met only briefly four years before. We were married after a short courtship and, thirty-one exhilarating years later, we are still together. God is using our hands for His purpose. Our work frequently takes us into the community and we continue to help people. We've also had our share of travel. You could say we are almost gypsies.

I had never met a real gypsy before, nor have I met one since. Rosa was refreshingly unique–positively one of a kind.

by Laura Lagana, RN

[*EDITOR'S NOTE*: For further information contact the **Michael J. Fox Foundation for Parkinson's Research**, Web site: http://www.michaeljfox.org.]

THE DEEP END by Matt Matteo

Reprinted by permission of Matt Matteo.

Touched by a Patient

As a nurse working in an acute-care surgical intensive care unit, I found myself caring for an elderly woman who was particularly afraid during her hospitalization. She completely rejected all attempts by the nurses to provide nursing care. She almost seemed unresponsive toward any efforts, on our part, to care for her, and she refused to speak, or even to open her eyes, when the nursing staff came into her room.

So intense was her fear that it was necessary for her daughters to be by her side almost constantly, in order to convince her to cooperate with even the most basic nursing interventions.

During this same period of time, I was suffering from a crisis in my personal life. Like my patient, I was also afraid and depressed. The genuine caring I normally gave to my patients was being distracted by my own pain and personal turmoil.

One morning, when I entered this woman's room to give her a bath, I knew from the other nurses that she would, under no circumstances, allow me to perform this task. Quietly, without uttering a word, I walked slowly to her bedside, taking her hand in mine in a gesture of honest caring and comfort. As I stood there for a few moments, peacefully holding her hand, she suddenly opened her wide, brown eyes. We were looking straight into one another's eyes. With a wrinkled smile that reflected years of wisdom, she said, "You are so sad. Trust in God and in yourself. Everything will be all right."

I was astonished that she could see the anguish I had tried to hide deep within my heart. My eyes instantly filled with overwhelming tears of tenderness and appreciation. I will never forget how this fearful patient was able to encourage and comfort me during my attempts to provide caring and comfort for her—this angel who was afraid of hospitals but not of caring.

by Jacqueline Laporta O'Kane

Jacqueline Laporta O'Kane, RN, MSN, CRNP, CLNC, is an Emergency Room Family Nurse Practitioner and Certified Legal Nurse Consultant. She is the single Mother of two children. She can be reached at 5507 Doral Drive Wilmington, DE 19808; e-mail: Okanejml@aol.com.

The Gift that Makes the Difference

Learning is a treasure that will follow its owner everywhere.
~ Chinese Proverb

"Why do you want to be a nurse, Patricia?" Two nursing instructors and the Dean of Nursing (the board of inquiry) sat facing me, looking me squarely in the eyes. I sat up tall in my hard, straight-backed wooden chair, feeling very small before them.

The Dean's voice echoed across the room. "Two thousand young people have applied to our program, and we will select sixty of them. Tell us why we should choose you." She folded her hands securely on the stack of application forms, looking up at me from behind a tiny pair of glasses perched precariously on the tip of her nose.

I wondered what the other applicants had said as they sat in this very chair. As I hesitated, I tried hard to imagine what they wanted to hear from me. My reason for wanting to be a nurse sounded simple and silly, so I remained silent in order to think.

My reason for wanting to be a nurse seemed laughable. As a child, I was terrified of doctors, nurses and hospitals. I dreaded every office visit, even for a check-up. But an incident from my childhood made me feel compelled to go into nursing, and I drew upon that experience for this board of inquiry.

When I was six years old, my parents were told that I needed to be admitted to the hospital for tests. They drove me to the children's hospital on a cold, gray Sunday afternoon in November. I looked up at the imposing building and quickly hid my face in my mother's coat sleeve. I tried to resist going in, but my mother and father were holding my hands. I was whisked along against my will.

We exited the elevator and my parents led me down a long hallway. We stopped at a large room that was divided into cubicles. We were directed to one of the cubicles by a stern, gray-haired nurse who pointed here and there, showing us where my suitcase should go, where my pajamas and robe should hang and other details.

My father went downstairs as mother tried to make me feel at home. The gray-haired nurse soon brought a supper tray, but I couldn't eat. Everything was different from what I was used to at home. My mother, picking at the food on my tray, tried to entertain me. She tried to cheer me up by telling me about some of the other children who were very sick, and how lucky I was to be there for testing. Soon I would be able to return home.

I wondered why my mother didn't have a suitcase too. *Wouldn't she need some pajamas and a robe?* After the nurse took the dinner tray away, I found out my parents were not allowed to stay with me. I had never been away from them before.

As my mother slipped into her coat, I began to cry. "No, no Mama! Please don't go! Please don't leave me!" I pleaded desperately. She smiled and tried to comfort me by saying she would be back tomorrow, to be a good girl and do what the nurses told me.

As her footsteps faded away down the long, dark hallway, I curled up into a tight little ball in my bed. I tried to think of the faces of my stuffed animals that lined the shelves in my bedroom back home. While deep in my thoughts, I was interrupted by another nurse who said firmly, "Time for bed." She helped me to change into a crisp hospital gown and I curled up into a ball once again. Feeling alone and frightened, I cried myself to sleep.

I was awakened during the night by fluorescent lights from the nurse's station that were shining in my eyes through the crack in the half-opened door. Someone came into my room as I lay whimpering in my bed. A soft, pleasant voice asked, "Aren't you sleeping little one?"

"I can't sleep. I miss my mommy," I cried. The soft voice coaxed, "Then why don't you sit up for a few minutes and talk to me."

"I want to go home." I began to cry again. The nurse with the soft voice pulled me toward her, holding me as I cried like a baby. "I think I'm going to be sick," I moaned, as my stomach began to unload its contents. She held a basin in front of me, and then gently gave me a sponge bath afterwards. She cradled me until I calmed down. I rested my head against her shoulder as she rocked me back and forth and I drifted in and out of sleep.

After what seemed like a long time, the soft voice said, "I have other children to look after. I can't stay any longer." As she gently laid me down on my pillow, I read her shiny name pin, "Miss White." I was so tired that I hardly noticed when she said goodnight.

My mother came to see me early the next morning, and the next night wasn't as difficult. Although I stayed in the hospital for only three days, I was grateful when that ordeal was over. I will always remember the loving kindness and compassion of Miss White, and how she comforted a lonely, frightened little girl.

As I sat before the board of inquiry, this incident finished playing in my mind. Sitting straight up in my chair and lifting my chin proudly, I began. "Being a hospital patient is a terrifying experience for anyone, although some are skillful at trying to conceal it. As a six-year-old child, I remember being hospitalized, feeling abandoned and terrified. A special nurse came to comfort me, and that is something I want to pass on to others. I want to be the one who cheers up a frightened child. I want to be the one who holds the hands of the lonely, the dying and the elderly."

That was the magic answer. On graduation night, I thought of Miss White. She would never know the profound influence she had on me. She taught me the importance of the gentle touch of kindness, empathy and compassion in easing the pain and anguish of others. Her gift to me was now mine to give back. The gift that makes the difference to our patients and to our world.

by Tricia Caliguire

Tricia Caliguire is a 1976 graduate of the Medical University of South Carolina's Allied Health program. She enjoys writing, public speaking, and partnering with her husband in their business. She can be reached at 529 South Parsons Avenue, Apt.603, Brandon, FL 33511; Telephone: (877) 573-0325; (813) 661-0237 (Voice Mail); Fax: (813) 661-7116; e-mail: Tcalig@aol.com.

THE DEEP END by Matt Matteo

Reprinted by permission of Matt Matteo.

Q-Ward

"What was that building used for?" Mary inquired, as we neared the end of our tour of the old state hospital grounds. I had shown her the buildings that housed the nursing school from which I had graduated many years ago. We saw the inpatient buildings, the gym where the graduation ceremony had taken place and some of the homes where the superintendent and doctors once lived. Mary, a psychiatric nurse with a keen interest in history, had only been inside the *new* psychiatric hospital that had been built in 1990.

"And that is Brown Building," I continued. "It was built around 1940 and was called home for four hundred women diagnosed with chronic mental illness. When I started nursing school, the hospital's census was twenty-seven hundred. I worked in Brown building several times, on different wards." As we concluded our tour I added, "The hospital has been in existence since the early 1800s and the nursing school was established in 1890."

This tour brought me back to my first day as head nurse, January 1967, just four months after graduation. They offered me Q-Ward in Brown Building because the sixty-five severely ill patients that lived in that particular ward made it difficult to interest most nurses to work there.

When I courageously started my new job, I discovered Q-Ward had been without a nurse for more than two years. A nurse would only go there to administer injections or draw blood—an obvious nurse-pain association. The aides ran the ward efficiently and had an established routine. It was only natural that, in the beginning, my presence would become equated with pain.

My job was cut out for me, and I was intensely aware that I would have to earn the trust of everyone, including the staff. I also brought with me all the naiveté and idealism of a new graduate. I wanted to fix everyone. Eager to practice new skills and to learn, I was ready to make a difference.

That first morning, I had difficulty unlocking the door to Q-Ward. My hands wouldn't stop shaking. As I surveyed the ward, I looked down both sides of the long, T-shaped, center aisle. On my right was the nurses station, followed by seclusion rooms, followed by several bedrooms. The corner room was assigned to Annie. Against the end wall was a large television, locked inside a screened box.

On the left was the entrance to the large, women's dormitory. Brown Building even had its own beauty shop, run by an amiable young beautician named Libby. She gave these women the ability to feel good about themselves. She made them all look pleasing.

Mrs. Vachon, one of the aides familiar to the patients, introduced me to everyone. "This is Miss Wing, our new head nurse." As we approached the corner room, Mrs. Vachon knocked loudly on the first door to make Annie aware of our presence. After knocking on the second door, Mrs. Vachon opened it carefully, making sure I was directly behind her, out of the line of vision at first. If Annie saw a nurse's cap, she was sure to have an angry outburst.

After I was introduced, I stepped up to the doorway and said, "It is nice to meet you, Annie. My name is Miss Wing. Please let me know if I can do anything for you." Annie looked at me, then began to swear loudly.

Annie's history was sadly interesting. She was first hospitalized in 1952. In those days, they photographed each admission, so I had the opportunity to see what she had looked like fifteen years before. Her face had a pretty but tortured appearance. She had a history of violence and, as a result, had two lobotomies and fifty shock treatments. There were stories that she required ten people to hold her down for an injection and to quiet her after one of her violent episodes.

I was determined to motivate Annie to come out of her room. For many weeks I repeatedly approached her room but didn't go in. Each day I gradually went in a little further leaving her door open for short periods of time. One day I noticed her sitting on a bench in front of the television. She only stayed out for a half hour that first time, but the duration of Annie's freedom gradually increased.

The staff started talking to Annie. Once, after I returned from lunch, I saw Annie playing cards with Mrs. Vachon. As I walked over to the card table, Annie looked up at me and asked, "Miss Wing, where's your cap?" Utterly amazed by her question, I realized that I had taken it off for lunch and had forgotten to replace it.

Annie added more to my surprise by saying, "If I were a nurse, I would never take off my cap." I don't remember how I responded, but I wanted to shout a triumphant "YES!" After many years of not speaking coherently, Annie had surprised us all.

One year later, I joined the Army Nurse Corp and prayed that Annie would continue to make progress. The dedicated staff continued their magnificent work.

I started my first day on Q-Ward with the intent to learn, and learn I did. Even if people show no outward signs of hearing or understanding, I speak to them as if they hear and comprehend anyway. I also discovered the beneficial effects of a positive attitude, and to treat people as I want to be treated.

These skills have continued to work for me over the years. Brown Building has been renovated and houses state offices, and Annie now lives in a group home within the community. I owe a lot to Annie and Q-Ward.

by Judith W. Magnon

Judith W. Magnon RN,c., BS, LADC is a certified Psychiatric/ Mental Health Nurse and Director of Assertive Community Treatment at The Mental Health Center of Greater Manchester, New Hampshire. Services include a Dual Diagnosis Team (Mental Illness/Substance Abuse), which helped her become a Licensed Alcohol and Drug Counselor. Judith has also participated in research with the Dual Diagnosis population. She can be reached at 67 Donahue Drive, Manchester, NH 03103; Telephone: (603) 625-1933; (603)668-4111 ext. 5217; e-mail: Magnonju@mhcgm.org.

The Lesson

You can gain strength, courage and confidence by every experience in which you really stop to look fear in the face. You must do the thing which you think you cannot do.

~ Eleanor Roosevelt

As a new and inexperienced nurse, I repeatedly found myself in uncomfortable circumstances that inevitably became significant learning experiences. While working in psychiatry, very early one morning, I was assigned to be medicine nurse. After carefully reviewing my procedures, my preceptor cleared me to finish giving a round of meds on my own.

With premature confidence, I approached the first patient's room. The door was slightly ajar, so I stepped into the darkened room and reached for the light switch. Instantly, I felt an eerie, uneasy sensation in the pit of my stomach. My feeling of confidence was quickly replaced by twinges of concern. Finally, my fingers found the switch and the lights came on.

"Good morning, Amy," I said, as I glanced around the empty room. Cautiously, I walked further into the room, carrying the small tray of medications intended for my elusive patient. All that remained in her bed were partially torn sheets and wrist restraints, still fastened and dangling from the bed frame like wilted flowers.

My heart raced as I looked around the room for my patient. I was keenly aware of her presence, even though I couldn't see her. The words of warning from morning report echoed in my head. *Amy is a notoriously elusive young woman plagued by addiction. Watch her carefully.*

With wide eyes, I glanced around the room. My knees began to tremble. This Houdini-like patient was obviously an expert at disappearing. Amy somehow managed to slip out of her restraints that were intended to protect her from fierce withdrawal symptoms.

Despite her young age, she was smart—and I was too naive to know what could possibly happen.

As I turned around, I saw a shadow out of the corner of my eye. Appearing from out of nowhere, stood Amy—right in my face. I gasped. Her glazed eyes were fixed intently on mine. Then suddenly, without warning, she grabbed for my throat. Consumed by panic, I let the medication tray crash to the floor as Amy's powerful hands began to close firmly around my neck, squeezing me in a vise-like grip.

Surely I was going to die. I could barely breathe as Amy squeezed harder. Staring into her zombie-like face, my mind raced for answers. Knowing I couldn't make a sound, I used my eyes to communicate with her. I prayed that I could reach her—and then I prayed for a miracle.

As I looked into her wild eyes, it seemed like we were connecting. Somehow I was reaching her. I felt an overwhelming fondness toward this poor girl. Her life was slowly being extinguished by dependency, and now she was about to snuff out my life. Using my eyes, I tried to express these feelings. Although her grip loosened only slightly, and she seemed focused upon my eyes, I still couldn't speak. I was biding time—grateful just to be able to breathe.

My mind raced as I prayed. *If she intended to kill me, she already had her chance. Her mind and body are reacting to the withdrawal of chemicals . . . Please God . . . help me do the right thing!*

Finally, her grip loosened a little more, giving me the chance to catch a short breath. In a raspy voice, I said, "Amy, you don't want to hurt me. You know I won't hurt you. I like you. Please let me go, Amy. I'll help you."

While I waited for her reaction, I asked myself, *After all, didn't I become a nurse to help people? Fine situation I got myself into this time.* Then her hands tightened around my throbbing throat once again. I expected to lose consciousness. *How could I have been so careless?*

Fighting back tears up to that point, I quickly lost control. As my tears flowed freely, Amy unexpectedly released her grip and melted into my arms, crying and trembling like a lost, frightened child who had just been found by her mother. "I like you too," she sobbed, resting her head on my shoulder. We cried together for a few minutes, before I guided Amy back to bed.

While I regained my composure and finished coughing, we talked for a few minutes. I explained the reason for putting the restraints back on her wrists, assuring her that she would have a better chance of recovery if she cooperated and followed the treatment plan. I walked out of her room, took a deep breath and said a silent prayer of gratitude.

As her therapy progressed, Amy told me about her turbulent life. She probably felt close to me because we were almost the same age. I learned that she hadn't heard the words, "I love you," since her older sister, Julie, died in a car accident. Amy's Mother had died years before in childbirth, while giving birth to Amy.

Finding herself alone with an abusive, alcoholic father, Amy couldn't cope any longer, so she ran away from home. Unable to find a job, she turned to prostitution to provide money for food and chemicals. Adopting the life of the streets, she tried to numb her pain with drugs and drink.

Amy's only real need was for unconditional love. We learned a great deal from one another during our brief time together. She recalled the importance of Julie in her life, and the power of sincere, genuine love.

Eventually she enrolled in high-school, and we lost touch. The social worker said that Amy was progressing well in her rehabilitation and studies, even working part-time at the deli around the corner. Although I still sometimes wonder where she is, and how she is doing, I cherish what I learned in the process.

by Laura Lagana, RN

One of the Finest Teachers

Learn to get in touch with the silence within yourself, and know that everything in life has purpose. There are no mistakes, no coincidences, all events are blessings given to us to learn from.
~ Elizabeth Kubler-Ross

I was working my first twelve-hour night shift on my own as a new nurse. It was a forty-two bed surgical unit for patients with ear, nose and throat (ENT) conditions, as well as patients that had plastic or oral surgery. We would often have a wide variety of patients with very serious and sometimes potentially life-threatening conditions.

Such was the case with Mr. Collins that night. He was an elderly gentleman who had been with us before, and had received a *hemi-laryngectomy for throat cancer. To help him breathe he had undergone a *tracheotomy.

Mr. Collins was admitted because they had discovered, on routine follow-up, that his cancer had returned with a vengeance. The tumor was just millimeters away from eating through the jugular wall. He was placed on special precautions and close observation and insisted on being made a "Do Not Resuscitate" (DNR) patient. Mr. Collins wanted his door closed at all times. He didn't want to be on display. I needed to monitor him closely, so we compromised—the door was closed only halfway.

Later that night, as I made rounds, I sensed something was wrong. As soon as I opened the door, my mind couldn't comprehend what I was seeing. I couldn't believe my eyes. Mr. Collins was seated calmly in his chair—legs crossed, head resting in his hands, a hat perched on his head—in an enormous pool of blood. I noticed another bloody puddle on the floor, under his chair.

Immediately, I grabbed some gauze pads and held pressure around his tracheotomy. I yelled for my medic to help and for the secretary to call the intern on-call, and his superiors, including the surgeon of the day.

I really wasn't sure of what to do next, but Mr. Collins remained amazingly calm. He was telling stories of his family and his experiences. I was struck by the familiarity of it all. His hat was a perfect match to one that was my grandfather's favorite. In fact, his demeanor and stature were astonishingly similar to that of my grandfather.

Just then I heard all three doctors coming toward the room. One of them grumbled, "This better be damn good!" The secretary directed them into the room, the senior followed by the two juniors. I watched as their faces did a repeat performance of mine. The senior asked for a brief report and the DNR status. I gave it all to them while maintaining pressure on the tracheotomy. They stepped out of the room, had a brief discussion, and then returned.

The senior swallowed hard, cleared his throat, and said, "None of us have actually dealt with this kind of situation before. Has the ENT on-call been notified?" I answered affirmatively. "Well then, until he gets here, just do what you think will help."

The medic and I just looked at each other and then back·at them. "Excuse me?" I said in utter shock and disbelief.

"You heard me Lieutenant," he snapped. "You're the ENT nurse. I'm a general surgeon. We don't see much of this sort of thing, and this gentleman has already decided he doesn't want resuscitative measures. So, just do what you think he'll need." He quickly turned and walked out of the room, leaving only one of the interns. The medic and I were appalled.

I applied what I had learned and it worked. Mr. Collins was trying to tell us all about his life. He used very simple words, nothing dramatic. I was amazed at his courage in the face of death. That night, I prayed for the first time, in a long time. I asked God to help guide me as I cared for this patient.

It was a long and exhausting night. I listened to my inner voice and trusted my instincts as I worked to keep Mr. Collins as comfortable as possible. I didn't move from his bedside the rest of the night. I believe no one should die alone. As I prayed that he would see his family one more time, they arrived early that morning. He died peacefully later that day, just after his family shared their good-byes.

I learned a lot about myself that night, and about dealing with the process of dying. It was an experience that I will never forget. Mr.Collins was one of the finest teachers I ever had.

by Susan C. Bailey

(*Hemi-laryngectomy: *removal of half of the larynx, the organ of voice.*)
(*Tracheotomy: *surgical opening into the trachea, or windpipe, for insertion of a tube to maintain an open airway and relieve obstruction.*)

Susan C. Bailey, RN, BSN, is a registered nurse. After earning her BSN at Northeastern University in 1991, she served as a Nurse Corps Officer. She is Chief, Allergy/Immunizations/Travel Medicine Clinic, DTHC, The Pentagon. She is involved in community crime prevention initiatives, and believes one person can make a difference and be a force for change. She can be reached at e-mail: scbailey@annapolis.net.

CHAPTER 3
REFLECTIONS OF GRATITUDE

Gratitude is not only the greatest of virtues, but the parent of all the others.

~ Cicero

Attitude Adjustment

Our attitude toward life determines life's attitude towards us.
~ Earl Nightingale

The day wasn't going well at all. We were extremely busy, as usual, and everyone was "on edge." We weren't actually short-staffed, but the number of nurses on duty that morning couldn't keep up with the steady barrage of chest pains, lacerations and kidney stones. To top it off, I was verbally attacked by a staff physician. I was trying to provide appropriate care to a patient who had been waiting for more than four hours in our emergency department without being seen by a doctor.

I was upset at the physician, the system and my own lack of power in this chaotic, uncertain world of the emergency department, where the only constant is uncertainty coupled with perpetual decision making.

Finally, at eleven o'clock, there was a small break in the action. "I'm going to get something to drink. Anybody want anything? I've been trying since seven-thirty and haven't made it yet. I'm going now." Quickly, I leave the noise behind, the "bells and whistles," and enjoy the solitude of the hallway.

Suddenly I see two ladies walking toward me. They look disheveled and tired, and both are dressed in wrinkled shorts and T-shirts, with straight hair in desperate need of a shampoo. They look as if they are going to say something to me. I am bad at remembering names.

A timid voice breaks the silence, "Ma'am?"

I look toward them. My face says, "Do you mean me?" I look at them still wondering who they are. "Ma'am, we just wanted to tell you . . . thank you for saving our mom's life the other day."

Just one simple sentence. That was all they wanted to share with me. My breath got caught in my throat and my heart skipped a beat. I saw my own mother momentarily flash through my mind.

The "garage code" was two days before–I had remembered it so well. I had even gone over it in my mind several times over the past two days. While standing at triage, I had seen the battered Ford careen into the garage, and a terrified, wide-eyed young woman jump out. As soon as I saw her, I knew it would be a "garage code." We don't usually save many of those–too long out without breathing and pulse. It's always so devastating for the family. Often our attempts are futile, but we always attempt to save a life.

I automatically geared myself up mentally for the challenge ahead. I saw the young woman's despair and ran to open the car door. My own heart raced. The patient stared straight ahead, her lifeless arms at her sides and her face ashen. Her limp dress conformed to the contours of her frail body and her chest failed to move.

As I screamed for help and grabbed the ambu bag, I pulled her out of the car and directed her two daughters to help me. We laid her on the concrete floor, and I placed the ambu over her mouth and nose. I started breathing life into the lifeless form lying before me, as I asked, "When did she stop breathing?"

"Just about three minutes ago–no longer."

I marveled at the precise answer. I repositioned her head, made a tighter seal and bagged again. Quickly a colleague was by my side. He felt for a carotid pulse–miraculously he found a faint one. We lifted her onto a gurney and raced to an exam room. Her monitor showed sinus tachycardia so we began administering oxygen.

The doctor was ready to intubate–the tube slipped easily into place. Respiratory therapy arrived and another nurse found a line. The fine art of crisis intervention accelerated our own actions, and the team came to life to save a life.

I talked to the family and apologetically explained the need to push them out of the way. I asked them about their mother's medical history. They said their mother had asthma, which had been much worse lately. They told me she started having trouble breathing the night before. I was grateful for the information. I could see their need for something positive from me as I put them in a conference room, so I called pastoral care and then returned to the business of triage.

The patient and family in front of me had witnessed the entire scenario as it unfolded, like an episode from a television program. They looked visibly shaken. I took a deep breath as I said, "Now, let's see what we can do for you."

"It's about time!" my new patient remarked.

I'll never forget those words. With my head bowed over the chart in front of me, I raised my eyes to the ceiling, took a deep breath and sighed. I politely took them to a room, but I couldn't smile–I just couldn't. I went on about my business of the day.

And now, out of the blue, two ladies bring me up out of the depths by saying, "Thank you for saving our mom." Of course, it wasn't just me, it was a team of finely trained professionals who go about the business of working together in harmony during a crisis. And when the crisis is over, we go back to the other patients who need us.

Isn't it funny how God works? Just before those two ladies appeared in the hallway, I was questioning, *Why do I do this? Why do I come in every day and go through the emotional roller coaster ride we call emergency care?* It's hard work and we rarely receive thanks.

So many lives quickly enter and exit. We touch their hearts and souls for a brief time and then move on.

Today I had tried to leave at seven-thirty, eight, nine–no way–too busy–not until eleven. Now my heart smiles and my step is a little lighter. I try to comprehend how I would feel if it had been *my* mom or dad. This is what it's all about. An attitude adjustment in disguise. A coincidence? I think not.

by Pat Clutter

Pat Clutter RN, MED, CEN is "Nurse-At-Large" living in Strafford, Missouri. She maintains a variety of positions: emergency nursing and house supervisor at a large trauma center in Springfield, Missouri; teacher at a local community college; writer and editor for publishing companies; a cruise-ship line nurse on board; and occasional flight nurse for a medical fixed wing service. She can be reached at 9361 East Farm Road 112, Strafford, MO 65757; e-mail: clutter@dialnet.net

Nurse Bonnie

Goodness is the only investment that never fails.
~ Henry David Thoreau

As far as I know, everybody just called her Bonnie. I can't recall her last name, but she was truly one in a million. Bonnie was a nurse on the second floor of the hospital in Washington State Penitentiary, Walla Walla, Washington, around 1971. She was one of those hands-on people. Whenever Bonnie talked to an inmate, she had her hand on their arm or shoulder, or she would straighten their collar. She always had time to talk to everyone—and she could talk! We all loved her, and it was very evident that she truly cared for us.

There was a big former heavyweight boxer, named Elmer, doing time with the rest of us. He had been shot in the forehead by a police officer. The bullet split when it hit Elmer, and it reduced him to the mentality of an eight-year-old, even though he was a giant of a man. The bullet caused such damage to Elmer's brain that he forgot how to read or write, and it also caused him to have terrible headaches when he forgot to take his medication.

These headaches often put Elmer into screaming rages. When this happened, the Goon Squad was called and he was taken to the hospital by force for his medication. The one thing Elmer never forgot was how to fight. He would put several of these specially trained guards on the injured list every time they had to subdue him.

I was working in the prison hospital one day when Bonnie came to my work area. She was leading a bashful Elmer by the hand. "Duke, have you met my friend, Elmer?" she asked. I knew enough about Elmer to stay as far away from him as possible. It was a well known fact that there weren't any two convicts in the place who could whip Elmer. I said that I knew him and hoped it would end there. He scared me, but it seemed everyone was afraid of Elmer, except Bonnie.

"Well," she said with a wink, "Elmer has a problem. He lost his glasses so he can't read or write very well. He has a letter from his daughter that he has been carrying around in his pocket for more than a month, but he's too bashful to ask anyone to read it for him. I want you to read the letter to him, Duke, and help him answer it. Will you do that for me?"

What could I say? The poor guy was ashamed of not being able to read so I read the letter to him. It was from his daughter, and she had recently had a baby. She wanted to know if Elmer wished to see some pictures of his grandson. She also wanted him to arrange things so she could come and visit. It had been almost thirteen years since she had seen her father.

When I finished reading the letter to Elmer, Bonnie started making a big fuss over it. "Elmer, you are a grandpa! Do you know that?"

Elmer smiled, his head wobbling from side to side. The scene was one for the books. Here was this tiny nurse bouncing around this huge, unpredictable convict. Bonnie was so happy she was just vibrating with joy, and pinching Elmer's cheek as she teased.

After Bonnie left, Elmer and I started to answer the letter. Elmer leaned over to me and said in a low voice, "Maybe ya can read it 'gain ta me 'cause I don't hear too good neither."

I read the letter to him again and again. After each reading, Elmer would ask questions like, "How do ta baby know I'm his grandpa? Do ya think ta baby gonna like me?" After countless readings and questions, we finally answered the letter and enclosed a visiting form for his daughter.

In the weeks that followed, Elmer would bring any new letters he got to Bonnie, who would, in turn, bring him back to my work area. I really looked forward to helping him with his letters. I also discovered his gentle side, a side that Bonnie was so quick to see.

One day, while Elmer and I were working on one of his letters, Bonnie came in and sat down. After listening to us for a few minutes she asked, "Elmer, if you could have anything you wanted in here what would it be?"

"Oh, nothin'." Elmer answered bashfully. "I'm okay."

"There must be something you would like, Elmer." Bonnie persisted. "You think about it and tell me three things that would make you happier here."

A few days later Elmer came up to me in the prison yard. He told me if he could have anything it would be to watch morning cartoons on the television, have a job like the other convicts and get some Tootsie® Rolls. I related his wishes to Bonnie.

Bonnie went to the Watch Commander and talked him into giving Elmer the job of cleaning the television rooms on weekends. The Tootsie® Rolls weren't sold in the inmates' store, so Bonnie would bring in a few rolls for him every day she worked.

Elmer did his job well. He had his own mop and bucket locked in the janitor's closet. He was proud, and you might be surprised to see how clean the convicts kept things when they knew they had to answer to Elmer for any mess they failed to clean up.

Bonnie and I noticed that whenever either one of us had to go somewhere in the prison, Elmer followed. We were both teased about having a full-time bodyguard. Elmer was making sure no one messed with his letter-writer and Tootsie® Roll connection.

One day Bonnie heard, over the guard's radio, that Elmer was going berserk with another headache in Wing 4. The Goon Squad was called and the hospital alerted for possible injuries. Bonnie immediately ran to Wing 4, ahead of the others, to confront Elmer. She walked up to the front of his cell with a stern look on her face, scolding the raving giant, much like a parent would scold a young child who had misbehaved.

"Elmer, you just quit this and come over to the hospital with me right now! This is foolish, and if you don't settle down, I'm never going to give you another Tootsie® Roll." Bonnie certainly told Elmer, and by the time help arrived, she and her Tootsie® Roll bodyguard were already walking out.

Years later I came through the prison at Walla Walla once again. Bonnie was still there but about to leave for retirement. She had numerous changes in her life. Her husband had died, and her daughters were grown with families of their own. We talked awhile and when it came time for her to go, I asked, "Bonnie, have you run into any more Tootsie® Roll bodyguards lately?"

For the first time since I'd known Bonnie she was lost for words. She stared out the window and after a few moments of silence looked back at me. With tears in her eyes she said, "Wasn't he a little sweetheart?" Bonnie went on to tell me about how Elmer died in the late 1970's, a delayed result of the gunshot wound.

Nurse Bonnie was one in a million, and she truly cared, no matter who was hurt or hurting, whether we were convicts or not!

by Ken "Duke" Monse'Broten

Ken "Duke" Monse'Broten was born in Park River, North Dakota. He has three grown children, four grandchildren and a new great-grandchild. He has written numerous articles and short stories, as well as a book called *Messages of the Heart*, under his pen name Edward Allen Lee. His contact information is available at Web site:http://www.angelfire.com/de/lagana/contributingauthors.html.

THE DEEP END by Matt Matteo

Reprinted by permission of Matt Matteo.

LAGA

All in a Day's Work

He was admitted to emergency receiving and placed on the cardiac floor. Long hair, unshaven, dirty, dangerously obese, with a black motorcycle jacket tossed on the bottom shelf of the stretcher, he was an outsider to this sterile world of shining terrazzo floors, efficient uniformed professionals and strict infection control procedures. Definitely an untouchable.

The nurses at the station looked wide-eyed as this mound of humanity was wheeled by, each glancing nervously at Bonnie, the head nurse. "Let this one not be mine to admit, bathe and tend to . . ." was their pleading, unspoken message.

One of the true marks of a leader, a consummate professional, is to do the unthinkable. To tackle the impossible. To touch the untouchable. It was Bonnie who said, "I want this patient myself." Highly unusual for a head nurse—unconventional—but the stuff out of which human spirits thrive, heal and soar.

As she donned her latex gloves and proceeded to bathe this huge, very unclean man, her heart almost broke. *Where was his family? Who was his mother? What was he like as a little boy?* She hummed quietly as she worked. It seemed to ease the fear and embarrassment she knew he must be feeling.

And then on a whim she said, "We don't have time for back rubs much in hospitals these days, but I bet one would really feel good. And it would help you relax your muscles and start to heal. That is what this place is all about . . . a place to heal."

The thick, scaly, ruddy skin told a story of an abusive lifestyle: probably lots of addictive behavior with food, alcohol and drugs. As she rubbed those taut muscles, she hummed and prayed. Prayed for the soul of a little boy grown up, rejected by life's rudeness and striving for acceptance in a hard, hostile world.

The finale was warmed lotion and baby powder. Almost laughable—such a contrast to this huge, foreign surface. As he rolled over onto his back, tears ran down his cheeks and his chin trembled.

With amazingly beautiful brown eyes, he smiled and said in a quivering voice, "No one has touched me for years. Thank you. I am healing."

by Naomi Rhode

Naomi Rhode, CSP, CPAE, is an inspirational speaker for healthcare and corporate America. She is a past president of the National Speaker's Association, a CSP (Certified Speaking Professional), a member of CPAE Speaker's Hall of Fame (Council of Peers Award for Excellence) and recent winner of the Cavett Award, the organization's highest honor. Naomi and Jim are co-founders of SmartPractice, a marketing company in healthcare and real estate, parents of three and grandparents of twelve. She can be reached at SmartPractice, Telephone: (800) 522-0595, Ext. 214; e-mail: nrhode@smarthealth.com.

THE DEEP END by Matt Matteo

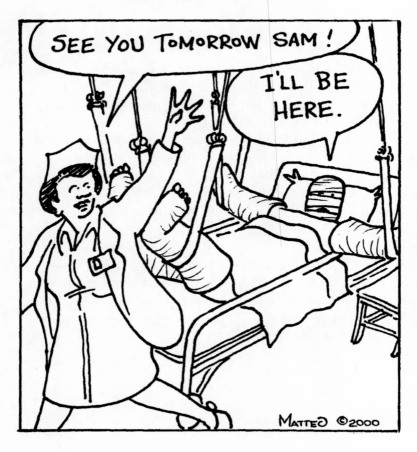

Reprinted by permission of Matt Matteo.

The Gift of New Life

I am a child of the 1950s—the last of the baby-boom generation and a registered nurse. I am also the youngest of four children, the wife of an only-child and the mother of one son. Other people may share some of these facts, but something else sets me apart from the rest—I am a cancer survivor—a nurse who has seen and experienced both sides of healing.

A little more than eleven years ago, I was busy racing through life, working part-time in a step-down unit, working full-time raising a four-year-old and setting occasional appointments with my husband in our attempts to have another child. Pregnancy didn't come easily for me.

One Sunday morning in July, 1988, my life changed. I awakened with a terrible pain in my belly and knew that something was wrong. Within days, I was diagnosed with Stage III Ovarian Cancer, after having my uterus and ovaries removed. Suddenly this ominous disease became my life—my story.

From there, I was led through an exhausting series of hospitalizations, surgeries and devastating chemotherapy at Mount Sinai Hospital, in Manhattan, New York. Throughout my experiences, many "angels" have touched me, although it has taken time and distance for me to see that.

On the first meeting with my oncologist, the room was crowded with the special people in my life—my husband, sister and parents. After the conference came the exam. When my doctor had a minute alone with me, he did something unusual. He took my face in his hands, and with a tender expression said, "You look like someone who doesn't want anyone to be mad at you." This was the first time since my diagnosis that I knew someone understood my loneliness. I cried. He was my angel of understanding.

Every three weeks I endured chemotherapy, with all of the unpleasant side-effects of nausea, intractable vomiting, complete hair loss and loss of independence. Too weak to work, or even to care for my family, it was hard for me to be the *recipient* of care. With time, I accepted my role and allowed many more "angels" to touch my life–each one played a major role in my recovery.

Rose, my head nurse, volunteered to do private duty for me on the first night of my surgery. She showed me that even a "boss" could be an angel.

My parents traveled a great distance to be with me after every treatment. They cared for me as they once did when I was an infant.

Susan, my loving sister, drove me from Long Island to New York City for my outpatient treatments, and practically carried me home from them all. She saw to it that my young son wasn't home after each treatment, so he didn't have to see his mommy be so sick.

The nurses from work, who are also my friends, helped care for my son and came to the hospital to be with me when I needed inpatient treatments.

During one early morning chemotherapy treatment, when I was sickest, one unforgettable nurse saw me wretching and crying. She said, "You have to start thinking of these medicines as your friends . . . friends who will help you get well."

At the time, I thought that her comment was mean and unsympathetic, but I was feeling sorry for myself. Now I know that it was her positive reflection on the demons that helped me through the agony and helped me to visualize the cancer being destroyed.

My husband held me when I cried. He never told me not to cry, even though it was hard for him to bear.

Our son never gave up on his mommy. To this day he is my angel–although at fifteen, he doesn't like to hear that. I thank God for helping me to see that having one child is precious.

I met many angels on my journey to wellness–each one touched me with the gift of new life.

by Jeanne O'Neill

Jeanne O'Neill, RN, BSN is a 1981 graduate of Adelphi University, Garden City, New York, and a member of Sigma Theta Tau International Nursing Honor Society. She is currently practicing in elementary school nursing on Long Island, New York. She can be reached at 348 Coolidge St., West Hempstead, N.Y. 11552; Fax: (516) 505-2168; e-mail: LTLPGS3@aol.com.

We Are Gifts to Each Other

Many years ago, when I was a student nurse, I remember a young boy on pediatrics who valiantly fought leukemia. He had been in and out of the hospital on many occasions, and the staff knew both the lad and his parents well.

He had been receiving treatment in the hopes of another remission, but it wasn't working and he lapsed into a coma. His mother came in each day and sat in a rocking chair next to the bed. After her son had been washed and changed, the nurses carefully placed him into her waiting arms.

After being unresponsive for more than a week, the young boy regained consciousness. While in his Mother's arms, he looked up at her and said, "I love you Mommy," then he closed his eyes and left this world.

I remember thinking how the staff's role *should* have been to console the grieving family, but it almost seemed the other way around. The Mother and Father had already come to terms with the fact that there might not be another remission, but the staff had not. *After all, wasn't it their job to find a cure and defend against death?*

The boy's mother and father consoled the staff. The parents shared how they couldn't have asked for a more beautiful way for their angel to leave them. They shared their deep faith and their love with all of the nurses they had come to know.

As nurses, we are sometimes called upon to be the giver, the server and the nurturer—and sometimes we must be willing to receive, to be served and to be nurtured. No matter our role, we must be open to both, to be whole again. We are gifts to each other.

by Lynn Durham

Lynn Durham, RN, is the mother of three sons, an author, monthly columnist and speaker for people who want to cherish and celebrate life. A creative antidote to anger, anxiety and anguish, Lynn presents Mind/Body/Spirit programs for stress hardiness and light-hearted living. Lynn helps individuals to gain the insights to choose the best strategies and tools to improve the quality of their personal and professional lives. She can be reached at: Telephone: (603) 926-9700; Web site: http://www.lynndurham.com.

Comforting Words

Just before Christmas, in 1998, my life took an abrupt detour. While I was attempting to clean the gutters along the roof, one last time before winter, I climbed almost to the top of the ladder when it suddenly began sliding down. *SPLAT!* The ladder crashed to the driveway with me still clinging to it. Lying there motionless for several minutes, with my eyes closed, I took inventory of my body-parts to determine if I were still alive.

As I raised my head, I felt a sharp pain in my left hip and saw what used to look like my left wrist, deformed and crushed, trapped behind the metal ladder, pinned against the driveway. Somehow I managed to free myself, put the ladder away and limp my way into the house. I waited patiently for my wife to return home from the grocery store.

After we made the necessary series of visits to the emergency clinic, x-rays, family doctor and orthopaedic specialist, the final verdict was surgery—early the next morning. At fifty-four years old, I had never had a broken bone; nor had I ever been admitted to a hospital, not even as an out-patient.

At the hospital, the staff busily scurried around preparing me for my early morning out-patient surgery. I scarcely knew who these cast of characters were until a man in a green scrub-suit arrived. He introduced himself as the Rotating Nurse. Once he made sure that everyone had completed their responsibilities, he wheeled me to the operating room.

On our way, he explained everything that I needed to know about my surgery. I felt extremely nervous and vulnerable. When I told him that my legs were shaking, he said, "You have a right to be nervous. You don't do this everyday, but we do. So you can rest assured that it's okay."

Those caring words were exactly what I needed to hear as I drifted off to sleep from the medication. Later, when I awoke in the recovery room, the first thing I remembered was the Rotating

Nurse's comforting words. That morning he was my "Angel of Mercy."

I never had the opportunity to learn his name, to personally thank him, and to tell him how much his soothing words meant to me . . . until now. Thank you, Mr. Rotating Nurse, and to all medical staff who help comfort their patients. I appreciate you and your compassionate care.

by Tom Lagana

Tom Lagana is a professional speaker, author and professional engineer. With more than thirty years' experience, Tom has worked with corporate clients throughout the world. He is co-author of *Chicken Soup for the Prisoner's Soul* and *Chicken Soup for the Volunteer's Soul*, a member of the National Speakers Association and 1994 recipient of the Jefferson Award for Outstanding Public Service. He can be reached at Success Solutions, P.O. Box 7816, Wilmington, DE 19803; e-mail: Success@TomLagana.com; Web site: http://www.TomLagana.com.

Home Care

"The nurse is here."
And I walk into someone else's life.
I hear the relief of, "Help arrived."
The hope that, somehow, all will be well.

"The Nurse is here."
And I see the pain,
Not only of my patient,
But of those who live with my patient.

"The nurse is here."
As I assess, plan, intervene, evaluate,
There is a communion, a sharing,
An understanding beyond words.

"The nurse was here."
As I go away again,
I hope that I have made a difference.

"The nurse was here."
When I call, later, on the telephone,
Just to be sure, I hear,
"It worked wonderfully. She is asleep."

Then I know I made a difference,
And I can sleep, too.

by Charlotte Iliff Lafean

Charlotte Iliff Lafean, RNC, BSN, is retired from full-time nursing after fifty years, and is self-employed on a part-time basis as substitute school nurse, home health aide instructor and insurance examiner. She loved her nursing career, the reason she continues to dabble in nursing related areas. She can be reached at P.O. Box 1115, Mcafee, NJ 07428; Telephone: (973) 209-4077.

LAGA

Threads and Transformations

My husband and I now refer to my episode almost jokingly. After being admitted to a psychiatric unit, I was advised to attend "group" and resist isolating myself. Weeks earlier, I had registered dismay at my diagnosis of depression. An incomprehensible fear and dread of living engulfed me.

To say that I wanted to die would understate the pain I experienced. More accurately, I wanted to no longer exist–to stop being. Numb and confused, I found myself next to a basket of wool fleece. Angelo picked some up and placed it in my hand, along with a wooden spindle.

I pretended to be somewhat interested so I wouldn't appear uncooperative. I wanted to push it away, creep off, curl into a ball and be alone. Surprisingly, with Angelo's good natured persistence, I was soon changing the thick fluffy mass into thread by pulling on a section of wool and turning the spindle. The task required coordination, organization and cooperation of mind and body.

The yarn often broke as I lost concentration or rhythm. The spindle would crash to the ground, and each time I began to think it was too difficult for me, Angelo would appear and say, "See, it's easy to reattach when that happens." With humor and patience, he would always repeat the same explanation until I could manage. Many times I would have given up if it weren't for Angelo's diligence. Through many faltering moves and despondent moods he kept teaching, encouraging, devising and fixing.

One day I made an error which stalled my progress. As I sat and brooded, Angelo appeared and reconfigured the spindle technique. The solution spared me the disappointment of failure. I picked up the thread and continued. My outlook was never quite the same. I thought, *If only I could just learn to rework a thing or two in my life with such artistry.* I resolved to try.

A transformation had begun. While passing through my fingers, the thick fuzz became a slender, continuous fiber. I noticed how my energy was transferred to the thread: too anxious made it skinny and tight; too morose made it fat and loose. The synchronized motion and feel of the yarn was pleasant. I started feeling good. During the activity sessions I began to feel more coherent, purposeful and optimistic.

Pharmaceuticals notwithstanding, Angelo's spindle became my turning point. As my mental outlook improved, I began to notice more around me. I observed Angelo moving among the patients, calming the agitated and encouraging the distraught with a profound respect for each person's dignity and individuality.

While Angelo tried to teach me to weave with my meager thread, I was learning how skillfully he could weave. In one session he took loud, demanding Jane, sat her down and placed paint brushes in her hands. Totally absorbed, she silently painted a landscape.

Angelo moved on to another, and while hovering over Mary's dull tree-scape, he asked, "Did you know that Jane used to be an art teacher?"

After a few moments of silence he asked, "Jane, how do you paint the tree trunks so that they don't look flat?" It wasn't long before an inspired Jane was seen instructing the younger, highly-strung Mary in a new skill. Jane had become quieter, more considerate and helpful. Mary became calmer, curious and more focused. What a transformation.

Angelo is special. He is a nurse in every fiber of his being. He treats the patients in his care with a gentle, caring compassion, consideration, patience, respect and intelligence. He not only made me *feel* better, he actually *made* me better. As a specialty, Angelo works through the medium of music to heal the sick, proof enough to me that music is the language of angels.

I recovered and returned to the realities of daily life, better able to cope and forever changed.

by Connie Shaw

Connie Shaw is a registered nurse. "I worked in Critical Care. I loved nursing the elderly, lonely and terminally ill patients but there was little time to provide essential care, let alone quality care, in today's healthcare environment. I am currently certified in Legal Nurse Consulting and work as a medical billing and contract auditor." She can be reached at e-mail: JohDynn@aol.com

My Guardian Angel

Example is not the main thing in influencing others. It is the only thing.

~ Albert Schweitzer

My guardian angel's name was Andrew, and interestingly enough he was a former patient of mine. He came to see me after my car accident when I had been moved up from the intensive care unit. To this day, I still don't understand just how he knew about my accident, but there he was. After a few words of greeting, he pointed his long, wrinkled finger at me as he said, "You look kind of skinny. Aren't you eating?"

I replied, "No. I don't care if I ever eat again."

With that comment he continued. "A very wise person once told me that it takes a lot more calories for healing when you are sick. Be sure and listen to your nurses now, and do what they tell you so you can go home that much faster."

I am convinced that what goes around comes around. Andrew's words were the exact words I had spoken to him while he was my patient. He made me promise that I would eat all my food from then on, and I did. I couldn't set a bad example for one of my patients.

Andrew's visit was short and sweet. He looked worried until he asked the nurse about my condition and when I would be well enough to return to work. As he prepared to leave, he leaned over my bed, touched my hand and said, "I hope they take good care of you. Don't forget to eat now."

I thanked Andrew for coming to visit me and we said our good-byes. He walked out the door stopping just as he reached the hallway. He hesitated and then came back to my bedside. I could see tears in his eyes as he spoke. "If I ever have to be in this hospital again I want you to be my nurse."

He turned quickly and was gone. His healing words are still with me.

by Jeanne M. Alford

Jeanne M. Alford, RN, is passionate about being a staff nurse and loves doing one-on-one teaching with the students. She also has a passion for Healing Touch. "My patient's personal requests will be honored if at all possible. I have worked at Memorial Hospital in South Bend, Indiana for nineteen years and love being a staff nurse." She may be reached at 545 7th Street, Mishawaka, IN 46544; Telephone: (219) 257-3862; e-mail: AJAlford@aol.com.

Please Don't Let Me Die

Gratitude is the heart's memory.
~ French Proverb

An eighty-eight-year-old female patient was admitted one night, during the 11-7 shift, while I worked in the critical care area of a medical emergency room, in a large metropolitan hospital.

That night I cared for five patients on stretchers, as well as several who were sitting in "asthma row" receiving inhalation therapy for acute asthma attacks. My work area was on the opposite side of the nursing station, a location that made me feel isolated. The patients on stretchers all had major cardiac irregularities except one who was unconscious and on a ventilator.

Among those five stretcher patients was "my angel," old and fragile. She must have weighed all of ninety-five pounds soaking wet and was only half the size of the stretcher. She was quietly observant despite the fact that she was having chest pain and the tracings on her electrocardiogram showed dangerous irregularities. Her paper thin skin bruised easily, and the resident doctor had difficulty gaining access to her veins.

The man on the stretcher next to her started having life-threatening irregular heartbeats which I couldn't stop. I initiated chest compressions and one of the resident doctors rushed over to help me. We moved the patient to the resuscitation room and desperately tried to break this terminal rhythm. Our efforts were futile. The fifteen minutes that we actually worked on him seemed more like hours.

I was upset to find that my work area had filled up with new patients during those fifteen minutes. An emergency medical technician student desperately attempted to help me, but I didn't need a student. I needed a nurse. These were the words I used to address my head nurse, who was across the open room. I also told her I needed help. This was absolutely crazy!

While talking to my head nurse I glanced up at the cardiac monitor above the lady who had previously complained of chest pain. She was continuing to have premature ventricular contractions and it was obvious the Lidocaine was not going to work. She grabbed my hand after I finished taking her blood pressure, and as I turned around to respond, her face said it all. A sense of calm came over me.

"Please don't let me die," she pleaded. Her entire body was shaking as she reached out to me with both hands. "Please don't let me die," she repeated. I looked at her face. Her hand was in mine and I stopped everything. I wiped away her tears and placed her hands in mine as I told her, "Don't worry. You're not going to die on my shift. We have too much work to do yet."

A light came over her as a smile came to her face. She said, "We don't want that now. We have lots to do yet." Then we both laughed. She watched me through the remainder of that shift. Every once in a while our eyes would meet, and we would both chuckle.

At the end of my shift she was still there, alive and kicking. She had been granted a bed in the coronary care unit and the student was collecting her belongings for her departure. For one last parting remark, she leaned over the stretcher, motioning with her hand for me to come closer, and whispered, "I'm sure glad that *you* were with me tonight."

You could say that both of us were caregivers that night. "My angel" is still with me. She sits on my shoulder each time I near the breaking point.

by Arlene Hanon

Arlene Hanon, RN, BS began her twenty year nursing career in 1979 as a Licensed Practical Nurse. "Nursing has been the stability in my life. I am the mother of two, one with diabetes and the other with Graves' Disease. Several years ago I sustained an injury at work and only recently returned to nursing. I know a positive attitude will help me succeed." She can be reached at 8905 SW 75 Street, Miami, FL 33173; Telephone: (305) 271-1514; e-mail: monda@bellsouth.net.

You're One Thought Away from Feeling Better

Change your thoughts and you change your world.
~ Norman Vincent Peale

As a new graduate nurse, working on a busy general and chest surgical unit in the early 1970s, it was almost impossible to get everything done on some shifts. One day, however, I managed a few minutes with an older gentleman who had just had his second above-the-knee leg amputation. He asked me, "Why doesn't God just let me die?"

I sat down, rested my hand on his arm and listened. He recounted heartaches and named physical challenges he and his other family members faced. He railed against God as to why He would put so much disease and difficulty into one family. He stated that he felt he was no longer enough of a man to live with so much of his body missing.

I'm not sure what I said, but I gave him the gift of listening and being present to him. I remember asking him if he had children and grandchildren–an inspired thought no doubt. It was memorable because, as he told me about them, his whole manner shifted and he beamed. It had seemed a remarkable change at the time.

Most likely I would have had a clearer recollection of those few minutes had I realized how important they were to this man at the time. I probably wouldn't even remember it all today, decades later, if it hadn't been for the fact that he walked over with his wife from the rehabilitation tower to see me, weeks afterwards.

He came over on two artificial legs to thank me for saving his life. He reminded me of the day I sat by his bed and listened. He told me that I was instrumental in his desire to live.

What did I do? Nothing special. I know it was only for a few minutes. I wonder how many times I have missed an opportunity of allowing myself to be used to be help someone heal their life.

How little is asked of us at times. Just to take a few moments with a listening ear and an open heart to make a difference.

I wonder, *How I can use the power of my thoughts to change my own life?* Focusing with gratitude on what we have left can help us to feel better and can make our world a better place.

by Lynn Durham

Lynn Durham, RN, is the mother of three sons, an author, monthly columnist and speaker for people who want to cherish and celebrate life. A creative antidote to anger, anxiety and anguish, Lynn presents Mind/Body/Spirit programs for stress hardiness and light-hearted living. Lynn helps individuals to gain the insights to choose the best strategies and tools to improve the quality of their personal and professional lives. She can be reached at: Telephone: (603) 926-9700; Web site: http://www.lynndurham.com.

Reprinted by permission of Lynn Durham, RN. Copyright ©1997 Lynn Durham.

As a British Lass Would

I have been a stamp collector since 1952, the year that my father died. I believe, to this day, that it was my Mother's way of occupying my six-year-old mind. Stamps were a way of letting my mind travel away from our Ohio home and the sadness that had engulfed me.

In my younger years, I would quickly get my homework out of the way so Mom could sit down with me and my stamps. We would use the world atlas to pinpoint far-off places, and then pull out just the right encyclopedia volume to read more about the people and places represented by those frail pieces of colored paper.

Many dreams and visions were placed in my stamp album during those formative years. Since then, I have examined and collected literally thousands of stamps, purchased in bulk lots to ensure many happy hours of looking through a mystery mix. It was in one such mystery lot that I came across a photo with a piece of paper wrapped around it. The paper, yellow from age and torn at the folds, protected the photograph like loving arms embracing a child.

I carefully unwrapped the brittle paper, and looking up at me was a young woman with the kindest eyes I have ever seen, besides those of my mother. The young woman was dressed in a Red Cross uniform that was almost floor length. Her half smile in that old black and white photograph clearly demonstrated that she took her job seriously.

She was proud of who she was, and what she stood for. As she posed for the photographer, with her hands behind her back, her posture told a story of an innocent young woman who was doing an important job in a troubled world wounded by war. She was a Red Cross nurse.

As I turned the photograph over, I discovered it had been printed in the form of a postcard. This was common practice during the early 1900s, as a way of sending messages back home to family and friends during the war.

The postcard didn't have a stamp or address on it, but in neatly written script was this chilling message, "In loving memory of Kitty, who drowned at sea on December 31, 1917. S.S. Osmanieh, torpedoed near Alexandria."

My heart skipped a beat as I turned the card back over to once again look at those kind eyes that were tragically closed at such a young age. *War was hell*, I thought. *What a loss.* But I wasn't the only one who thought this young lady had been taken from the world far too soon.

As I carefully unwrapped the paper that had been protecting the memory of this young nurse, I found another tattered piece of paper, tucked neatly inside. Someone had written a poem as a loving tribute to this young nurse. I wept as I read it.

The unknown poet must have felt the deepest love and admiration that one human being can have for another. This innocent young woman is a symbol of all of the brave nurses, women and men, who gave their lives in war; and they, as well as Kitty, should never be forgotten. Rest in peace, brave lady. Rest in peace.

by Steven Dodrill

Steven Dodrill is a fifty-something photographer-turned-writer out of self-defense from changing times. "I love life and the people in it. My purpose in writing this story is to truly remember the nurses that gave their lives in war. I guess I'm still an old sailor at heart." He can be reached at 86 Kendal Drive, Oberlin, OH 44074.

Photograph of Red Cross Nurse

My Little Friend

When I was eight years old my Mother took me to visit my dear friend in the hospital. The attention given my little friend, Emma, by the nurses and doctors, was very impressive. On the way home, I announced to my Mother, "I want to be nurse." After all, I was already doing laundry, as well as feeding and changing diapers for my newborn sister, Marie.

From that day on, I decided to work hard in school and concentrate on a nursing career. My parents had mixed emotions about my leaving the nest. I was the only one out of five children who wanted to move away from home, just twenty miles away.

My nursing career finally began when I entered the four-year program at St. Mary's Hospital School of Nursing, in Philadelphia. We were required to work and study twelve hours a day, six days a week under the guidance of well-trained doctors and Franciscan nuns. I thoroughly enjoyed every minute of that rigorous schedule.

It wasn't all work. We managed to have some fun. There were monthly dances with our friends and the interns. We used to play tricks on the new interns. Sometimes they would leave their jackets in the nursing station. When they returned they would find that the usual contents of the pockets, stethoscope and pens, had been replaced with an assortment of embarrassing unmentionables.

One night we called the intern to do lab work on a patient in obstetrics. When he arrived, he prepared to examine the patient. As he pulled back the covers, he found a large pillow and one of our student nurse's posing as a patient in labor. He was obviously displeased about being the object of our friendly prank. We howled and scattered in different directions when the elevator door opened, and out stepped our supervisor. The fun was over.

On another night, we hung a dummy out the window, making sure it was in full view of the intern's quarters. While it dangled on a rope, we made the dummy come to life by making it bob up and

AGA

down like a fish on a hook. We managed to intimidate a few interns in our day, and we also made some laugh.

When I graduated in 1934, during the Great Depression, jobs were scarce. We worked a twelve-hour shift for five dollars a day or a twenty-four-hour shift for slightly more—six dollars. We volunteered our services as "angels of mercy" for people who couldn't afford to pay.

While I waited to hear from the Pennsylvania State Board of Nursing that I had passed the state board examinations, I took on a six-month private duty nursing assignment for an elderly lady in her own home. I became a registered nurse while on that first assignment and many new private duty assignments soon followed.

The years have flown, and I can hardly believe that I'm now eighty-eight. I'm grateful for my good health, a wonderful, caring family and for my little friend, Emma. I now live in a beautiful retirement facility where I continue to volunteer my services as an "angel of mercy."

My reward is in the pure satisfaction of knowing that I have helped and cared for so many others. I live by, and use, these words to close every card and letter that I send: "Keep well, happy, and God in your heart."

by Catherine (Jennie Gilardi) Lagana

Catherine (Jennie Gilardi) Lagana, a retired registered nurse, was born and raised in Bristol, Pennsylvania. She enjoys playing cards, dancing, daily exercise, family and helping others. During her nursing career she taught home nursing, volunteered for the American Red Cross, was a private duty nurse and, many years ago, was nominated for Nurse of the Year. She can be reached at P.O. Box 7816, Wilmington, DE 19803.

THE DEEP END by Matt Matteo

Reprinted by permission of Matt Matteo.

CHAPTER 4
MODELS OF PERSISTENCE

When you get into a tight place and everything goes against
you, till it seems as though you could not hang on a minute
longer, never give up then, for that is just the place and time
that the tide will turn.

~ Harriet Beecher Stowe

Happy Birthday Grace

"It was a great birthday, Nancy," my mother said. "You're not
going to believe what Tina did."

Several months earlier, my father had been diagnosed with
Parkinson's Disease. This crippling disease progressed very quickly.
In the early stages, realizing that he was getting sick, Daddy asked
me for a favor during his first hospital visit. "Please take care of
your mother, honey," he begged. "That's all that I ask of you."

Within six months, Daddy was totally bedridden and the
majority of that time he couldn't speak above a whisper. His doctor
held my hand and broke the news to me. "Your father will not get
better, Nancy. It's all downhill from here."

Unfortunately, the doctor was right. Our entire family was
heartbroken, as we slowly lost Daddy to this horrible disease. I
thought I was prepared for the storms that were ahead.

I did pretty well until the holidays and other special occasions
crept up on us. I really dreaded my mother's birthday. I knew how
hard it would be for her. Although I bought her a present from
Daddy, I knew that things still wouldn't be the same for her.

Since I lived seventy miles away and couldn't visit every day, I called to check on both of them every night. I began to notice my mother's downcast mood a couple of weeks before her birthday, while we talked on the phone, but I never mentioned it. I didn't know what to say.

Daddy had resided in the nursing home since the previous year. Fortunately the nurses and their assistants knew Mom well. Tina, one of Daddy's nurses, sensed my mother's lack of joy and enthusiasm. Somehow she found out that my mother's birthday was drawing close. I am grateful to her for going beyond the call of duty to lift Mom's spirits on her special day.

Tina bought a small picture frame with a little tape player inserted at the bottom that could hold a brief message. She placed Daddy's picture carefully inside the frame. Daddy still had the capability of speaking in a faint whisper with a great deal of coaxing. For two solid weeks, after my mother left the nursing home for the day, Tina went into his room and begged him to say "Happy Birthday, Grace" into the microphone.

A few nights before my mom's birthday, Tina managed to get Daddy to speak. She was so excited that she ran up and down the halls of the nursing home playing it for all the employees to hear. His voice was very faint, but the words were very clearly spoken, "Happy Birthday, Grace."

On her birthday, like she did every other day of the year, Mom went to see Daddy. Sitting on his lap was a beautifully wrapped gold box. Happy birthday balloons adorned every corner of the room. Tina slipped into the room right behind my mother, along with some of the other employees.

When my mom opened her present and pushed the tiny button, Daddy's voice could be heard saying softly, "Happy Birthday, Grace." It was a moment that my mother will always remember. Tina not only took care of my father, but she also took it upon herself to take care of my mom's emotional needs as well.

The tone of my mother's voice, as she told me the story, let me know that we were surely going to make it through the trying days ahead. And it was all because of a nurse who took time from her busy schedule to care about things like the love between a sick man, his wife and birthdays.

by Nancy B. Gibbs

Nancy B. Gibbs, a weekly religion columnist and freelance writer, has appeared in *Honor Books* and *Guideposts Books*. She has been published in several magazines including, *Angels on Earth*, *TWINS*, and *Christian Reader*. She is a pastor's wife and mother of three grown children. She can be reached at P.O. Box 53, Cordele, GA 31010; e-mail: Daiseydood@aol.com.

[*EDITOR'S NOTE*: For information contact the **National Parkinson Foundation, Inc.**, Bob Hope Parkinson Research Center, 1501 N.W. 9th Avenue, Bob Hope Road, Miami, FL 33136-1494; Telephone: (305) 547-6666; Toll Free National: (800) 327-4545; Fax: (305) 243-4403; e-mail: mailbox@parkinson.org; Web site: http://www.parkinson.org.]

A Basket of Roses

We must become the change we want to see.
~ Mahatma Gandhi

It was the first time I heard it—the cry of an unseen child. There I sat at a stop light, disgusted. At the age of sixteen, I looked for work that allowed me to enter into the profession to which I was drawn like a magnet. Yet, after visiting two geriatric nursing homes, I sat in my green Thunderbird and recalculated my plan. The nursing homes made me sick. The smell of urine was squelched only by thick cigarette smoke. I sat at the traffic light alone, watching the pulsing of traffic across U.S. Route 20, and feeling overwhelmed. That's when I first heard it.

Quiet but persistent, distant but mysterious, it was the unmistakable cry of a young child. A cry for help. I turned down my radio, opened my window and heard it again, but not clearly. I threw my car into park, got out and walked around the back end, peering into the ravine just to my left. The people in the cars behind me had either not heard the child, or decided their time was too precious to wait, so they drove around me. No child. No clues.

Back in my car, I sat puzzled. Traffic continued to race past me as my gaze settled on a small, nondescript one-story brick building, kiddy-corner from my view. On the front sign were the words, "Elaine Boyd Creche," and the picture of a cradle. Finally, a green light, and I began turning left, only to hear the voice again. I turned immediately into the parking lot of the brick building and tried to compose myself.

I had heard about this place—something about mentally retarded children who rode tiny, yellow buses and sat with their distorted faces pressed against the dirty glass, smeared with saliva and sweat. Maybe the voice belonged to a child here. I needed to find out. The heavy, steel door sighed as I pulled it open, and the darkness that enveloped me was split by the light that streamed in through a small, wire mesh window behind me.

"Are you here for an application?" a woman asked. I nodded silently. "Do you know what kind of children we have here?" I nodded again.

"I want to be a nurse." The words trickled out. I was hired on the spot and became the newest nurse's aide in a snake pit–a snake pit of angels.

Of the one-hundred and thirteen children at the Creche, I was drawn to a small, misshapen child, nearly six months old. Fair and blonde, deaf and blind, Kim was given up at birth by her fifteen-year-old mother who had tried to terminate her pregnancy in the second trimester. Kim, born earlier than everyone would have liked, was spared death but wore her mother's guilt as cerebral palsy.

Day after day I spent every spare moment caring for Kim, kissing her and rocking her as I listened to the stories of the more experienced aides. They knew the other children well.

Layla's mother had taken LSD throughout her pregnancy, leaving Layla with one eye in the center of her face and a mouth that stretched across the side of her head. At three, she would cry if she saw her reflection in a mirror.

Ricky, a fourteen-year-old boy whose contorted muscles tightened like a vise around him every waking moment, was left to spasm on a floor mat all day. He could talk, but he usually cried. There were so many more–orphans, wards of the state or children with families who could not bear the pain of caring for their imperfect gifts.

What was hardest for me to bear were the conditions. No diapers, only ragged towels draped the bottoms of the children. We washed the towels by hand in a large sink at the end of each hall. I had feces under my nails. There was no air-conditioning, and in the middle of the Chicago summer the smell of the place escaped into the parking lot.

But I had Kim, and she knew me. When I held her she would

roll her eyes, as if trying to see past her thick, white corneas, to catch a glimpse of the young girl who played Mom. I would bathe her in my own baby products and dress her in clothes that I bought with my own money. I would rock her to sleep before heading home at 11:30 p.m. to begin my school work.

My parents became Kim's foster family. She was able to come home with us every evening and spend the weekends. I was thrilled that Kim had found a place in my family and in the hearts of my parents.

But I was troubled. *What about the others?* I wondered. My aunt suggested that I pray, so I did. I prayed for a chance to help all of the children. Little did I know my answer would be waiting for me the next day.

A neighbor who heard me talk about the Creche and the conditions of the care had asked me to contact a friend of hers— someone who might be able to help. A reporter for ABC-TV, Peter Karl, was in the throes of investigating geriatric nursing home conditions, but he agreed to talk to me. I told him everything— how the facility ran out of food at times, the sanitation, and the staff physician who falsified his visits.

The next day, I had a candy bar wrapper with a camera hidden inside. I was to journal everything I saw, heard and did. I agreed to stay on at the Creche for a year, working for ABC and the Better Government Association. He wanted a story.

We both wanted something good to happen. It did. Our exposé on the facility was nominated for a Chicago Emmy award, but most of all, my prayer was answered. Because of the publicity, state nursing home laws were changed to help ensure the safety and care of disabled children, previously a loophole in the system. Although the facility never shut down, it was cleaned up.

We had Kim for ten years. During that time, I became a nurse and a journalist. Although she never walked, she taught me to stand tall. She taught me to speak up through her silence; and in her pain, she taught me that we are all brothers and sisters who must care for each other.

I had a special dress made for my flower girl, Kim—one just like my wedding gown. She was supposed to be pushed down the aisle in her wheelchair; but instead, I was forced to say goodbye in a hospital emergency room. My little sister died of pneumonia. A basket of pink roses sat on the altar as a reminder that she would always be with me in spirit. I have heard her voice many times since then and continue to respond.

by Carrie Farella

Carrie Farella, RN, MA, is the corporate writer for *Nursing Spectrum Magazine*, Hoffman Estates, Illinois. She can be reached at (847) 438-6675; e-mail: CLFarella@aol.com, or CFarella@nursingspectrum.com.

Angels Called Nurses

They were angels of mercy in a time of pain,
To care for the wounded on an endless train.

They came as young ladies, not a line on their face,
Their youth long gone, old age took its place.

This was their job by what life would inject,
But what they saw, they just didn't expect.

Only at night do they shed a tear,
Thank God this duty is for only a year.

One after one they came and they went,
With each beat of the heart another was sent.

As a river flows in a raging flood,
So did the floors with a soldier's blood.

Her emotions well hidden, dare never be shown,
She could only let them go when she was alone.

War is hell and can be unforgiving,
But she can only help heal the scars of the living.

The look on their faces that death was near,
A gentle hand took away that fear.

Their hearts were broken in a myriad of tears,
How could a legless man finish his years?

A gentle touch . . . a whispering word,
For the blinded boy will forever be heard.

It was a difficult time, situations were crude,
Only in a glass of wine could she find solitude.

She returned in the morning to an empty bed,
She knew deep in her heart he was better off dead.

Every day in combat was a year more you age,
Every gray hair earned was earned out of rage.

The women of combat are just as brave,
They honor the boys, the ones that they save.

They were the tamers in a lion's den,
Who dare say they were not as strong as men.

The soles of their feet were covered in blisters,
It broke their hearts when they lost their sisters.

In her dreams under halos of grace,
She remembers their names and knows every face.

Their minds are heavy about the carnage they saw,
They will not let their sons fall to another war.

Of all the pains I had to embrace,
There was no better cure then the smile on her face.

She said we would make it, she was so damn sure,
We wouldn't be here if it wasn't for her.

They should feel no guilt, only their pride,
They were angels called nurses, they stood by our side.

by William L. Gallagher
Suggested by Louise Riel, RN

William L. Gallagher served in the Vietnam war. Writing poetry is his way of thanking all who dedicated their lives to caring for those wounded in the war, as well as in memory of all who were unable to return. He can be reached at 4 Village Rock Lane, Apartment #4, Natick, MA 01760; Telephone: (508) 647-4055.

Gutsy Nurses

Nurses are the real heroes of medicine.
~ David Letterman

We finally made the agonizing decision to remove the life support from my seventeen-year-old son, who remained in a state of constant seizures, despite heroic medical interventions. Our family waited at his bedside as moments turned into hours and then eventually into days. It was in the first hours of my most feared and private parental nightmare that I was blessed with a gutsy, merciful pediatric nurse.

Palliative levels of medications prescribed to calm Damon's seizures, as his life ebbed away, were clearly not enough. For the most part, his level of consciousness was not clear, and for those of us standing vigil at his bedside, the sight of his body retching with constant seizures was nearly unbearable.

When the pediatric intensivist (physician specializing in the care of critically ill children) on duty that first evening refused to consider a change in the medication order, I was left in numbing shock and disbelief. Both the attending neurologist and the intensive care staff had promised us that what we were experiencing at that moment would never happen. It was at that dark moment, unbelievably devoid of compassion, that the gutsy nurse walked in.

I can't remember if I was able to verbalize effectively, but she seemed to understand. She looked around the room, listened and then disappeared. Within minutes, she was back with an order to increase the medications that allowed Damon to appear more peaceful and relaxed.

Unless one has experienced the slow, painful death of a child, over a long period of time, it is difficult to understand just how special this nurse's compassionate action was to us.

Apparently our son's nurse had broken the rules and called the "highest authority" at home, in the evening, to advocate for my son and our family. Thank God she was gutsy enough to take that assertive action and professional risk for our son. There aren't enough words to describe how grateful I am and how much that one act of kindness, gutsiness and mercy affected me. She was action oriented and highly motivated in her nursing values and beliefs.

I don't know that nurse's name, and I never saw her again. I do know, however, that during Damon's last week of life he was more at ease, and our moments together were more tender, because of that merciful nurse who was on duty one evening, when a child was dying.

Now I am a nurse, and I believe that gutsy nurses, like the one who placed herself in the line of fire for Damon, are what it will take to meet the changes facing healthcare today.

by Fran Abell

Fran Abell, RNFA, CNOR, a Registered Nurse First Assistant in surgery, was finishing her last semester in nursing when her seventeen-year-old son died. "There isn't a day that goes by that I don't think of my son. The experiences are a reference point for every major decision, value and belief I have. In memory of my son and a classmate, a scholarship fund was established at the University of Maryland School of Physical Therapy." She can be reached at 8218 Londonderry Court, Laurel, MD 20707; Telephone (301) 317-5353; Fax (301) 317-8174; e-mail: Trahey10@msn.com.

The Other Side of the Mountain

Fall seven times, stand up eight.

~ Japanese Proverb

Only thirty-two more miles to go, Kathy thought as she drove home on that icy October night. She was a tall, pretty woman in her early forties, a real head-turner with long, dark, shiny hair and silky, smooth skin. Extremely tired, sporting dark circles under both eyes, Kathy was more than eager to get home to bed. As part of her nurse's training, Kathy had been working with patients at a Denver hospital since two o'clock that afternoon. Her day had begun at five that morning with study and preparation for clinical experience.

As Kathy drove, she reflected on her dream of becoming a nurse. It was not an easy decision to return to school after staying home and raising five children. This was the subject of many late night discussions with her husband, Jim. They had been married for twenty-five years, and the added stress of school, long hours away from home and coming in at odd hours were serious considerations.

Kathy felt grateful to be so close to becoming a registered nurse. Nursing school had provided an exciting but exhausting challenge. As she drove home that night, she relived her memories of those last three years.

The first year she earned excellent grades, except for Pharmacology. School officials required her to repeat Pharmacology *and*, in order to remain enrolled, the entire first year. It was a difficult and humbling experience, but Kathy studied harder than ever and completed all of her studies successfully. That was only the first mountain she would have to climb during her nursing education.

Soon after that, Kathy was suddenly confronted by a much

larger obstacle. While driving to class one morning, running late as usual, Kathy noticed that, in her haste, she had forgotten to wear her seat belt. Slowing down to quickly fasten her belt, she looked up again and saw flashing lights from police cars along the side of the road and two policeman clearing an accident.

The next thing Kathy remembered was waking up in the passenger seat of her car. She couldn't see anything. Every movement caused excruciating pain. Terrified, she tried to gather enough strength to call out to the voices she heard in the distance. She must have passed out again because the next time she heard voices they were louder and closer, accompanied by the sounds of tools prying the car door open.

Kathy recalled very little of the ambulance ride, but she remembered her prayers for God's help. The next sound she heard was the sweet sound of Jim's voice. She held out her hand, and he came over to embrace it. *Thank God Jim is here*, she thought. *Now everything will be okay.*

She drifted in and out of a pain-drenched fog, receiving meticulous care from the trauma staff. The doctors ruled out a possible ruptured liver and internal bleeding. Kathy knew she was lucky to have survived, even though she sustained a concussion, fractured facial bone with some nerve damage, three broken ribs, a sprained wrist and multiple contusions.

Jim phoned the nursing administration office to inform them of the accident. He discovered that, if Kathy missed more than one week of school, she would have to drop out and start over. Kathy felt angry and betrayed. She couldn't understand why she wasn't receiving the same compassion that she was being groomed to give others. After only four and a half days in the hospital she was released. Kathy prayed and reached deep inside herself to find the strength and courage to return to school.

There were many obstacles that she had yet to face. Because she couldn't focus her eyes for more than ten minutes at a time, studying for her upcoming test was extremely difficult. Her classmates made audio-tape recordings of their notes for her.

The day Kathy walked into the room to take her test, she was wearing large sunglasses to cover her severely bruised and swollen face. She removed her sunglasses and approached the lady administering the test. Kathy told the woman about her accident and why she would most likely need more than the allotted fifty minutes. Without taking her eyes off of Kathy's face, the woman touched Kathy's hand and told her to take as long as she needed.

As Kathy sat down with the test before her, she didn't dwell on passing but on finding a way to focus her eyes. She held the paper up to eye level, read the question and closed her eyes to think about the answer before she opened them again; this helped to minimize the dizziness created by reading. Each question was answered in the same manner, and she finally finished more than one hour later.

Kathy knew she had finally reached the other side of the mountain when she earned an "A" on her test. During the next several weeks, she overcame many hardships. She made the honor roll and landed a job in a Denver area hospital.

On her journey, Kathy discovered she was capable of doing far more than she thought possible, by tapping into her faith and inner strength. She is an example of tenacity and courage. She knows who she is, what she wants in life and where she is going. Colorado has the Rocky Mountains, the Cowboys and a courageous nurse by the name of Kathy Chambers.

by Shirley Doan

Shirley Doan is a contributing writer for the *Julian News*, in her hometown. Her first love is writing. "The Other Side of the Mountain" is a true story of her daughter. She can be reached at P.O. Box 1047, Julian, CA 92036; Telephone: (760) 765-2679; e-mail: shirleyd@abac.com.

THE DEEP END by Matt Matteo

Reprinted by permission of Matt Matteo.

A Tour of Duty

The country was being torn apart by the Vietnam War, and nurses were being challenged to provide an array of services in Vietnam, as well as state-side. I went into the Army Nurse Corps in October 1967, with all of the innocence, naiveté and idealism of a young nurse who had lived her entire twenty-two years in New Hampshire. The idea of traveling and being an officer was intriguing, but I worried that I wouldn't be accepted. Little did I know that, as long as I was a nurse of the right age, weight and was breathing, I was "in."

Basic training occurred at Fort Sam Houston in San Antonio, Texas and included a week of "field training" to prepare us for duty in Vietnam. Only sixteen out of the three hundred and fifty nurses in my basic training class didn't go to Vietnam at some point.

My favorite part of training was when we were assigned, in groups of four, to go from point A to point B on a map, using a compass and a point-man system. Our group stayed on task, and we almost made it to the exact spot. A number of nurses had to be "air evac'd" out by helicopter, after not showing up for hours, because they were distracted by the cows in the fields.

My tour of duty took me to San Francisco, California for six months of training in Psychiatric Nursing, then on to a Psychiatric "air evac" center at Fort Gordon, Georgia. Only active duty personnel were treated there, and most were twenty-four hours out of Nam. My eighteen months there challenged all of my psychiatric nursing skills, while affording me an invaluable learning experience from a number of talented people; especially one young psychiatrist who had been drafted three months before, completing his residency in Pennsylvania. Fortunately for me, he loved to teach and would instruct anyone who wanted to learn how to provide services and interventions to those suffering from mental illness.

There are many stories about the lives that touched mine, and here is but one.

AGA

It was another hot, sunny afternoon. I was supervising the three-unit psychiatric wing, located at the back of an old World War II-type hospital, with units lining the long corridors. There were miles of corridors and many units. I can still picture the green floors and hear the creaking of the doors, just as they did on the day when a young soldier came dashing in to update me on a new admission.

"He's dangerous, and he's mute . . . he's also in a straight jacket," he reported.

I couldn't believe my ears. "A straight jacket?" I asked.

"Yes, Ma'am," he answered.

I had never seen one, despite having been trained at a state psychiatric hospital, nor did I see one again. As I went out, he opened up the back of the enclosed truck to reveal a frightened young man on an army stretcher, covered with a blanket—heaven knows why. It must have been 110 degrees inside that truck.

My heart was wrenched and my nursing skills kicked in. Immediately, I removed the blanket and called him by name. "Joe, if I take off your straight jacket, do you have enough strength to walk into the unit?"

He answered, "Yes," so I removed that awful thing as fast as I could and assisted him inside, where he was given food and fluids. This was only the beginning of many months of psychiatric care for this young soldier.

Joe was solitary and non-verbal for days, but a consistent, caring and respectful approach from all the staff, combined with medications, began to engage him. One of the ironic developments that I discovered, as I began to work with these young soldiers just out of Nam, was that I had to be a *nurse* first, and an *Army* officer (Lieutenant Wing) second; otherwise I could not engage them and build up trust quickly, and without it they couldn't or wouldn't share their experiences. Years later, I realized that they were only protecting me and the other staff from the true horrors they had seen and dealt with.

The actual "break through" with Joe came quite by accident

one day when he overheard me and a young male corpsman talking about the TV show, "Star Trek." I loved the show and was very animated as I analyzed the most recent episode. After a while, Joe came over and started to talk about his favorite episode and characters. As we discussed the show, our therapeutic relationship was sealed and his recovery process was hastened because he was able to break his silence. Trust was established so he could share with me some of the horrors he experienced while serving as a solider in the trenches of a foreign world.

Soon Joe was able to share with other staff and his peers. He began to participate in group therapy and individual sessions with the Psychiatrist. He joined in on the social activities, which included movies on the unit. He never did become assaultive as implied by the presence of a straight jacket upon his arrival. These interventions led to his being discharged to home and family with follow-up care.

To have Joe smile and say goodbye clarified the reason why I had become a nurse. Any nurse reading this account will truly understand what I mean. Each of us has one of those days when we're blessed by the gift of "touching someone's life" in a way that helps to heal a wound—regardless of the type.

My tour of duty ended in October 1969, with mixed feelings. I had never shed a tear for all of those stories that I had heard. I thought I had dealt with it and had gone on with my life. The reality of the situation caught up with me ten years later in a movie theater in New Hampshire.

My sisters asked me to go with them to see *Home Coming*, so I did, thinking it was some type of unpretentious movie. It turned out to be about a Vietnam veteran coming home in a wheelchair. The audience sees the war through his eyes, as well as through the eyes of his friend's husband. I cried during the movie and for three straight hours afterwards.

My poor sisters didn't have a clue what was happening to me. I was usually calm and in control. Suddenly I understood exactly what a "flashback" was. When I walked out of the theater, I expected to see the psychiatric wing at Fort Gordon in front of me—with all the staff and young soldiers there—and it would be 1969 again. It was also difficult for me to see the Broadway show, *Miss Saigon*. I had seen most of the "in country" Vietnam war movies without a problem. I didn't expect this.

There are so many stories in my head about those young men. I was privileged to have worked with them. To this day, I often wonder how their lives turned out. *Do they have the happiness they deserve? Have the ghosts gone for them?* How I wish I could tell each one of them how much they touched my life during my tour of duty.

by Judith W. Magnon

Judith W. Magnon RN,c., BS, LADC is a certified Psychiatric/Mental Health Nurse and Director of Assertive Community Treatment at The Mental Health Center of Greater Manchester, New Hampshire. Services include a Dual Diagnosis Team (Mental Illness/Substance Abuse), which helped her become a Licensed Alcohol and Drug Counselor. Judith has also participated in research with the Dual Diagnosis population. She can be reached at 67 Donahue Drive, Manchester, NH 03103; Telephone: (603) 625-1933; (603) 668-4111 ext. 5217; e-mail: magnonju@mhcgm.org.

A Whole Person

The future belongs to those who believe in the beauty of their dreams.

~ Eleanor Roosevelt

Our son was born with a complex congenital heart defect. Over the last nineteen years, Stephen has required open heart surgery four times. He has also been hospitalized many additional times for ongoing complications, and each time an "angel of mercy" has reached out to us. Our "angels of mercy" have not only touched us—they have also encircled our lives with continuous compassion, tender care and endless support.

Choosing only a few examples of how these nurses have opened their hearts to our son is almost an impossible task. At the age of three months, Stephen had his first cardiac catheterization. His nurse gave me her stethoscope because she knew that I was anxious about having to check his heart rate at home.

During one of Stephen's more recent hospitalizations, his nurses cheered upon hearing the news that his senior finals had been waived, making him an official high school graduate. During our journey, we have never had to be alone.

After his third surgery, Stephen had to be rushed back to the operating room because of a massive chest infection. Nurse after nurse came to his bedside, as they left their shift, to tell us they were praying for him.

When he was experiencing yet another crisis, one of his day nurses, Ginny, suspecting something was amiss, called in at around ten o'clock that night. Upon finding out that Stephen was battling a serious infection, Ginny came back in and sat by his bedside. She stayed until well after midnight, comforting and reassuring us.

With each subsequent hospital stay, our son has grown to love the Children's Hospital of Philadelphia (C.H.O.P.) as his home-away-from-home. Some of his nurses have cared for him for years, and others have touched his life only briefly—but they have all helped him to learn to enjoy life, with all of its challenges, and to see the blessings he has.

When Stephen was young, these "angels of mercy" held him, hugged him, rocked him and felt his pain—they cared for him emotionally and physically. As he grew older, they laughed and joked with him, and talked with him about his life away from the hospital.

Stephen's nurses have helped to mend his broken heart many times over. Spiritually speaking, they have been our "angels of mercy." They have helped to make our son feel like a whole person—a person with a life and a future—a person with dreams to be realized.

by Sharen A. Resendes

Sharen A. Resendes is Stephen's mother. "Our son was born with hypo-plastic left heart syndrome, TGA and stenosis of the pulmonary artery and the mitral valve. Having developed a complication several years ago, he also requires tube feeding. His nurses have been wonderful. He is our miracle who attends West Chester University." She can be reached at 707 Wickersham Lane, Kennett Square, PA. 19348; Telephone: (610) 388-2368.

Reprinted by permission of Sharen A. Resendes. Copyright ©1998. Sharen A. Resendes.

[*EDITOR'S NOTE*: For information contact the **Children's Hospital of Philadelphia**, 34th Street and Civic Center Boulevard, Philadelphia, PA 19104-4399; Telephone: (215) 590-1000; Web site: http://www.chop.edu.]

The Last Dream

Dream as if you'll live forever and live as if you'll die tomorrow.

~ James Dean

As I reflect back on my nineteen years of pediatric nursing, there are many vivid memories of patients and families that have touched my life. From these special people, I have learned the meaning of love, dedication and strength. Their impact has been immeasurable–their wisdom has helped make me the nurse I am today.

It has been more than ten years since I have cared for Elizabeth. Her courage and strength will never be forgotten. She was twenty-two years old, had Cystic Fibrosis, and was in and out of the hospital five to six times a year for routine "tune-ups" or for treatment of respiratory ailments. Every hospital employee who had ever worked on the pediatric unit knew and loved her.

Her last admission lasted three months and is the one I remember the most. Elizabeth was in the final stages of this dreadful disease. She had deteriorated and required forty to fifty percent oxygen by nasal cannula to provide sufficient oxygen to her body tissues, and continuous *gastrostomy tube-feedings at night to combat anorexia.

When the mucous production increased, Elizabeth needed frequent chest physiotherapy. She began having more difficulty breathing and demonstrated severe shortness of breath. She was miserable and became angry with the staff.

I especially remember the day her pulmonary physician, Dr. Daniels, discussed end-of-life issues with her. He was honest with Elizabeth, explaining what would eventually happen and what her options would be–to be intubated to facilitate suctioning or to stay on high dosages of potent antibiotics and "wait-it-out." He further explained that long-term intubation might lead to a tracheostomy or eventual mechanical ventilatory support if her pulmonary function deteriorated.

Elizabeth became angry when she realized her options were

limited. She said emphatically, "I don't want to be kept alive on machines, and I'm not ready to die!" She wanted to fulfill her dream—the dream that many twenty-two-year-old girls have of getting married and having a family. She had been dating Kevin for almost two years, and although she knew what would eventually happen to her, she never really expected it.

Elizabeth told her doctor that she needed time to absorb everything they had discussed. As he stood up to leave the room she said, "Please close the door on your way out and tell them I don't want to be disturbed."

She cried alone for what seemed like hours. We desperately wanted to go in, but we also knew she needed her own space. Waiting was difficult. When she finally rang her call bell, I hurried to her room. She was curled up into a ball, hugging her favorite teddy bear. Her eyes were red and swollen from crying. I took her into my arms and we sat together arm-in-arm, crying.

Finally she whispered, "I don't want to die. I'm not ready."

As I sat and listened to her, I thought about the skills I learned in nursing school. *What could I say to her? What shouldn't I say to her? How could I help her come to terms with all this?* As these thoughts were racing through my mind, I remembered something one of my instructor's had said. "Above all, show your patients that you care. Be a good listener and stay with them, and don't be afraid to cry with them." That is exactly what I did.

When we were both "cried out," we talked. Elizabeth told me about her dream of marrying Kevin, walking down the aisle in a beautiful wedding gown and waltzing with him for the first time as man and wife. I knew what I had to do.

I called a quick consultation where we all discussed the possibility of facilitating her dream. Her doctor questioned Elizabeth's stamina. We knew her days were numbered and we had to work quickly. We discussed our plan with Kevin and Elizabeth's family, as soon as they arrived.

Kevin was elated about fulfilling Elizabeth's dream. We knew we had to work together to make the wedding date a reality. Several of us even volunteered our time.

Dr. Daniels treated Elizabeth aggressively over the next few days. He changed her antibiotics, increased her dosages and electively intubated her. We administered bronchodilators and provided chest physiotherapy every hour, followed by frequent suctioning. Her parents made all the arrangements for the ceremony.

Our goal was to help Elizabeth achieve her last "dream," and we did. She left the hospital on a one-day pass and became Kevin's wife. She returned earlier than planned, fatigued and needing prompt attention, but I will always remember the look of contentment on her face. As she struggled for air, she whispered, "Thank you . . . all!"

by Helen Papas-Kavalis

(*Gastrostomy tube-feedings: liquid nutrition given through a surgically created opening from the external surface of the abdominal wall into the stomach)

Helen Papas-Kavalis, MA, RNC graduated from New York University in 1979 with her BSN degree, and has worked exclusively in pediatric and neonatal nursing. Helen returned to NYU, completing her Master's Degree in 1985. She is certified in pediatric nursing and is Assistant Professor of Nursing at Bronx Community College, where she teaches pediatric nursing. Helen is also the mother of three. She can be reached at 214-24 45 Drive, Bayside, NY 11361; Telephone: (718) 229-6798.

[EDITOR'S NOTE: For information about Cystic Fibrosis contact **The Cystic Fibrosis Foundation**: 6931 Arlington Road, Bethesda, MD 20814; Telephone: (301) 951-4422 or (800) FIGHT CF (344-4823); Fax: (301) 951-6378; e-mail: info@cff.org; Web site: http://www.cff.org.]

Nurses on Horseback

When I became old enough to ask that all important question of Mom and Dad, "Where did I come from?" I didn't receive the usual answers like, "You were found under a cabbage leaf," or "The stork brought you." My answer was, "You were brought to us by the nurse in her saddlebags!" You see, I was born in Eastern Kentucky, at the foot of the Appalachian Mountains, as far up a holler as one can get. I was delivered by a nurse mid-wife of the Frontier Nursing Service (FNS).

The FNS was founded in 1925 by Mary Breckinridge, who dedicated her life to the care of the children of the frontiersmen. Many years before, while visiting friends in North Carolina, Mary looked helplessly on as a small child, who suffered from typhoid fever, withered and died. It was then that Mary began to consider a future in nursing.

After completing her nursing education, Mary studied midwifery in London. Later, she observed the work of the Highlands and Island Medical and Nursing Service in Scotland, which became the model for the FNS.

Mary chose to build her service of operations in the vastly forested coal country around Leslie County, Kentucky–a region of steep mountains and narrow valleys. There were no roads, as we know them today, and not a single licensed physician. Horseback and mule were the only modes of travel.

The center of Mrs. Breckinridge's operation was a large, log house at Wendover that was to be her home for forty years. This house, referred to as the "Big House," was located about four miles from Hyden, Kentucky, along the Middle Fork River. There was no access to the Hyden side of the river until years later. Even today, the narrow Wendover Road is not an easy drive and in some places one must cross a swinging bridge.

My mother's side of the family worked in Wendover for years. When there were buildings to be constructed or ground to be broken the word was carried up Camp Creek. There was never a shortage of help for the midwives and nurses.

I can still see my grandmother riding up the road on her horse from Wendover, as I sat on the rock wall. Times were tough, but when someone needed a nurse or midwife, no matter what the weather, the call was answered on horseback with forty-pound saddlebags in the old days. Today the horse has been replaced with jeeps and helicopters.

The "Big House" is still a special place. A new hospital in Hyden carries Mrs. Breckinridge's name. Come September, there are the Mary Breckinridge Days, which is homecoming for a multitude of babies that were delivered by the FNS nurse midwives.

Mrs. Breckinridge chose the Kentucky mountains because of their inaccessibility, creating a life-saving connection between modern medicine and people living in remote areas of Kentucky. She felt that if the work she had in mind could be done here, it could be duplicated anywhere.

Today, though the area is not as remote as in the past, the need for the Frontier Nursing Service and its forward looking approach to healthcare is as great today as it was in 1925. Thank you Mrs. Breckinridge.

by Clellon H. Callahan, Sr.

Clellon H. Callahan, Sr. was born in Leslie County, Wendover, Kentucky. He graduated from Ohio University with a BS in Antiquary. He has had poems and tall tales published in *Canto*, *Good Old Days*, *Reminisce*, and *Leslie County News* and is working on a book of poetry, *Then & Now (Vietnam & Prison)*. He can be reached at: 4704 Beechwood Rd, Cincinnati, OH 45244.

[*EDITOR'S NOTE*: For information contact **Frontier Nursing Service, Inc.**, Web site: http://www.frontiernursing.org; or **Frontier School of Midwifery & Family Nursing**, 195 School Street, P.O. Box 528, Hyden, KY 41749; Telephone: (606) 672-2312; Web site: http://www.midwives.org.]

Just a Nurse

We will find a rainbow,
And shine it in your eyes.
We'll hold onto empathy
And wear it in disguise.

Taking care of pain
With a smile or a pill,
We'll be there to heal
What diseases try to kill.

Using all our knowledge
To give your life a start,
When grief overwhelms you,
We'll serve you from our heart

When pain becomes unbearable
Or bad news you've been told,
We're a soft shoulder to cry on
Or a sturdy hand to hold.

When everything seems hopeless
And you don't know what to do,
Reach out and press your bell,
And we will comfort you.

Please call on us to help
Even if you are in doubt.
We'll stay by your side
When others have walked out.

Whenever you feel alone
And things are getting worse,
Only then will you understand
We are more than just a nurse!

by Judy Cook

Judy Cook, RN, BA is a psychiatric nurse and published author of the humor novel, *"If Life's A Party, Where's My Invitation,"* published by Winston-Derek Publishers, Nashville, TN. She can be reached at P.O. Box 512, Cedar Knolls, NJ. 07927; e-mail: judyful@nac.net.

CHAPTER 5
ACTING ON FAITH

Faith is to believe what you do not yet see; the reward for
this faith is to see what you believe.

~ St. Augustine

Tee-Off

An octogenarian golfer, Mr. Carter, could only walk the emerald
links in his memories when he was admitted as a patient to
our hospice program. An inoperable cerebral aneurysm had stolen
most of his sight and would soon steal all of his life. Before this
dark thief sneaked in on him, he walked and played at least thirty-
six holes of golf every day. He lived for golf.

This swinger of yesteryear had a birthday soon after his
becoming a hospice patient, and our volunteer staff was in a
quandary as to what they might do to help him celebrate his
birthday in proper fashion. One of the truly splendid things about
hospice is the recognition of important days for patients by staff
and volunteers; anniversaries, birthdays and holidays. Hospice
workers know all too well that these days probably won't occur
many more times for these patients.

The staff decided to surprise Mr. Carter with a luncheon at a
restaurant of his choice. What they didn't tell him was the nature
of dessert—a visit to the Picken's Country Club where a guided
tour of the course in a golf cart, with detailed explanation of the
course by an experienced golfer, had been prearranged with the
golf pro.

Following a fine birthday lunch, Mr. Carter, his nurse, social worker, home-health aide and the volunteer coordinator went for, what proved to be, a magical Tru-Flite experience. While an experienced golfer talked him through the course, telling him the distances on the fairways and the lay of the greens, Mr. Carter offered his suggestions on club use—a seven iron or a pitching wedge or putter. In his mind, he might as well have been at the Masters Tournament in Augusta with full galleries cheering him on.

At the club house, following his tour, Mr. Carter was given the opportunity to show he was still in swing with life. The staff that accompanied him to the country club maneuvered him to a putting green, guided his hand to the cup and let him step back his paces from there to challenge the others to a putting contest. He was virtually blind to this world, but in his dreams he could still see. He actually went on to win that small putting contest with the hospice staff.

That putting contest never made it to the annals of the PGA but did make it to the annals of Heaven where, no doubt, Mr. Carter has bragged about it often, but not as much as he did about his final exploit on the golf course.

About this same time, hospice was arranging a fund-raising benefit tournament. It was suggested that, if Mr. Carter were still alive when the tournament took place, he should be the one to hit the first ball of the contest. When he was told of this plan, one might have thought he had been told he was going to live anew as a successor to Arnold Palmer or one of the other golf greats.

Mr. Carter was excited. Every time a nurse or health worker went out to his house, they were quizzed on the status of the tournament. "Was it still going to happen? Would it be soon enough?"

Just before the great event it was announced that a special guest, Mr. Carter, would be hitting the first ball to open the tournament. By this time he was essentially blind and had to be led to the tee. A ball was placed for him. He was put in position, told where the ball was, given a club and allowed to follow his dream. He hit the ball more than one hundred and fifty yards, perhaps even one hundred and seventy-five yards, down the center of that fairway, as if it were laser guided.

"Did I hit it?" he asked. "Where'd it go?" The other contestants erupted in applause. For him, Augusta had arrived in time. He stayed for the whole tournament to see who would win. We already knew who the real winner was. The others just raised money. Mr. Carter raised our awareness of how real dreamers can do just about anything.

For the remaining days of his life, Mr. Carter could speak of no other thing than the magic of that Tru-Flite ball going down the exact center of the fairway.

"Call unto me, and I will show you great and mighty things which thou knowest not."

by Craig C. Johnson

Craig C. Johnson has traveled forty nations. Having faced possible early death from a terminal neurological horror, he saw his lifetime dreams shatter. He has faced death nine times. "Life has been more than good . . . it has been truly wondrous!" Medical researcher by day, Mr. Johnson creates illusion in community theater by night. He can be reached at P.O. Box 2404, Anderson, SC 29622; e-mail: Craigjohnson15@hotmail.com.

The Touch of Kindness and Prayer

Show kindness toward another in their troubles, and courage
in your own.

~ Princess Diana

It was one of those familiar situations where we were invited to
two parties on the same day. It was summertime, and everyone
was planning their barbecues and pool parties. Our friend's boss
was throwing his third annual pig roast, complete with disc jockey,
bartender, catering team, pool with a slide, boats and wave-run-
ners. Who would miss this one? So, with our two children in tow
and our friends accompanying us, we ventured to this gala affair
on a gloriously warm and sunny summer day.

The house and grounds were so magnificent that ten minutes
after we arrived and the older children were in the pool, we were
offered a grand tour. My six-year-old son accompanied us.

Immediately following the tour, we stepped out into the
backyard, my husband and friends proclaiming, "Let's go see the
pigs roast." As they turned to go, out of the corner of my eye, I saw
a fully clothed man make an impressive dive into the deep end of
the pool. I froze, thinking how unusual this scene was. At that
moment time seemed to stop.

I watched in shock as a limp, blue child was lifted from the
bottom of the pool. Screams of "Call 911!" and "Help me . . . this
child isn't breathing!" echoed through me, but I was already at his
side, shaking him and feeling for a pulse or a breath. I yelled, "I'm
a nurse, does anyone else here know CPR?"

There was no response to my plea, but having been in charge
of an emergency department for six years, fourteen years ago, I
instinctively knew what I had to do. As I cleared his airway and
prepared for CPR, I felt a tap on my shoulder.

Standing beside me was a strapping gentleman who stated, "I
was in the military for twenty-five years. I know CPR. If you tell

me what to do, I can help." So I landmarked for him, and together we performed CPR.

The scene was unlike the typical emergency room depicted on television. The child's eyes fluttered, and he began choking and spitting up. As we continued CPR, breathing and checking for a pulse, I was acutely aware of a man kneeling over us, hands extended. He was speaking and praying in tongues.

"Who are you?" I asked.

He responded, "I'm the child's father."

"Keep praying."

I was vaguely aware of a number of other things going on around me. The boy's mother had dialed 911 and was having a conversation with someone on a cellular phone, telling them what was going on. The bartender was running around hysterically screaming, "Help her . . . the child is dead!" My six-year-old son and eight-year-old daughter were immobile, wide-eyed and in obvious awe.

As the child began to regain consciousness, he murmured his name and age upon my request. I oriented him to time and place, and instructed him to stay still and to keep his head to the side. I promised him that I would stay by his side until the ambulance arrived. He looked frightened. His body was twitching and moving involuntarily. I asked someone for a blanket, turned him on his side and spoke softly into his ear to calm him.

I remember his mom coming over to me, handing me the cell phone and saying that the 911 staff wanted to speak with me. I spoke to an EMT (emergency medical technician) who asked the child's status and informed me that the ambulance would arrive momentarily. The EMT continued speaking with me, asking how I felt.

Unexpectedly, I broke into tears. "I used to run an emergency department . . . where is my airway, ambu bag and suction . . . he's still blue . . . he needs oxygen NOW!"

Within seconds the ambulance personnel arrived, established an intravenous site and started oxygen by mask. With a cervical collar in place they transferred the child from stretcher to van, his parents following behind them.

With lights flashing and sirens blaring, they quickly took off. SILENCE. As I looked around, I saw parents clutching their little ones. The older children were standing near the pool, too afraid to enter. Many wide-eyes stared my way. Slowly they walked toward me saying things like, "Thank God you were here."

The host and hostess hugged me. After expressing their gratitude, they cried and were very shaken at the thought of what could have happened had I not been there. Once calmed, I took the opportunity to be the "nurse" again; only this time, not the hands-on caregiver but the nurse-educator.

Child safety and advocacy is one of the issues that I deal with, in my work as a nursing administrator of a children's hospital. I cautioned the group that, since they live in an area that has numerous canals and pools, every neighbor should be trained in CPR. I suggested that nearby hospitals set up courses in CPR for the community. Finally, I quietly took the host and hostess aside and urged them to give careful consideration to providing a lifeguard for future social functions.

A short time later, the parents returned and asked that I accompany them to the hospital. The healthcare team in the PICU (pediatric intensive care unit) wanted to ask me some questions. But first, there was something I needed to do. I went up to my husband and reminded him not to let our children go near the pool or canal in my absence. Who would be there to help my own children if *they* should need aid?

It felt wonderful when I entered the PICU. The nurses and doctors assured me there was no evidence of neurological damage, and that the child should recover fully. He would be observed for the next twenty-four to forty-eight hours.

When I went to see him, he was sitting up in bed. With a big smile he said, "Thanks for saving my life, nurse." I was walking on air.

During the ride back to the party, I was convinced that I was meant to attend this particular party. I was definitely *sent* there. As we pulled into the driveway, the boy's Mom greeted me, tearfully expressing her desire to pay me back in some way. I turned to the boy's father and said, "As I worked on your son, I noticed you were praying in tongues. Where did you learn that?"

"I am a minister . . . a healing minister."

I moved toward him and we joined hands. Looking into his eyes, I confided, "Two months ago I was diagnosed with metastatic breast cancer. The best thanks you can give me is to go to your congregation and ask them to pray for me, pray for my healing and pray for a cure." We embraced and he promised to carry out my wish.

by Kathi Smillie

Kathi Smillie, RN, MPH, is an Assistant Administrator for Nursing at Schneider Children's Hospital of North Shore-Long Island Jewish Health System. She is responsible for the Neonatal Intensive Care Unit, Pediatric Medical/Surgical Unit, and Prenatal Care Clinic. "I have spearheaded many programs devoted to the development and well-being of children." She can be reached at 1308 Allen Drive, Seaford, NY 11783; Telephone: (516) 783-8023, or (718) 470-3381; e-mail: nurz21@aol.com.

[*EDITOR'S NOTE:* For information about first aid and CPR training, swimming and life-guarding programs, baby-sitters' training and more, contact the **American Red Cross** through your local chapter, or by accessing their Web site: http://www.redcross.org; e-mail: info@usa.redcross.org.]

The Touch of an Angel

"What is it?" I asked as I entered the kitchen and saw my dad sitting in a chair at the table, his head resting in his hands. I had stopped by for my usual Saturday visit, as I'd done every week since Mom's death. He glanced up. "I need to see a doctor. I don't feel well."

"But Dad, Dr. Halloway is out of town," I said. "He told you at church last week that he intended to spend Christmas Day fishing." One glance at my dad's ashen color, his mouth twisted in pain, and I knew he was right.

I reached for the phone and dialed the surgeon's number. I listened to the recorded response, then replaced the receiver. "It's Christmas, Dad, and the surgeon's office isn't open. I'll take you to the hospital emergency room. You've probably eaten something that disagrees with you. In a couple of hours you'll be feeling better." I helped him out of the chair and led him toward the driveway, where I'd parked my car.

On the drive to the hospital, I tried to keep the conversation light, talking about my two boys' activities at school. Dad nodded in response but I could see from his frown that the pain hadn't subsided.

Twenty minutes later, I pulled into the emergency entrance of the hospital. For two hours I drank coffee and exhausted the magazine supply in the waiting room while they examined him. With nothing left to do, I closed my eyes and began to think back to the last couple of visits that I'd made with Dad.

He had seemed well at the time, although I remembered him coughing. When I suggested he get it checked out, he reminded me that it was allergy season, and he already had enough allergy medicine to last a lifetime.

"Mrs. Riley," a deep voice said near my ear.

Startled, I opened my eyes and looked into the face of Dr. Luther, one of the physicians at Dr. Halloway's practice. "We're trying to get in touch with Dr. Halloway. In the meantime, I wanted to let you know we've examined your dad and we need you to sign some papers."

"Papers?" I mumbled. Then I noticed two pieces of white paper in his hand.

"You have to give us permission to operate."

"Operate? But Dad just ate something that didn't agree with him," I said. "He doesn't need an operation."

"I'm afraid his stomach trouble is a little more serious than that. The x-ray shows a dark spot. I'd like to take a look," Dr. Luther said.

As I sat in the waiting room, I listened to the rustle of the nurses in their crisp white uniforms as they walked down the corridor. Every so often an announcement blared from the P.A. system, breaking the silence.

Two hours later, I turned toward the sound of approaching footsteps. Hands in his pockets and a stethoscope around his neck, Dr. Luther strode toward me. A lump formed in the back of my throat. *Maybe Dad hadn't made it*, I thought. "He's okay, isn't he?" I blurted out.

"Mrs. Riley, your father is in intensive care. He'll be sleeping for the next couple of hours."

"Intensive care? But doctor, he's going to be all right isn't he?"

Dr. Luther wet his lips before speaking. "The next few hours will be crucial. We removed the cancer but his heart gave us a scare. How long has he had a heart condition?"

Cancer . . . heart condition? Unable to disguise my puzzlement, I said, "But Dad's never been ill. He visited the doctor for his allergies but I don't remember him ever being really ill." I couldn't control the thoughts running through my mind. *How could this happen to my dad?* "You did get the cancer . . . all of it?" I managed to ask.

Dr. Luther nodded. "We did. I'll be in to check on him later."

I thanked him and headed for my dad's room. As I entered and made my way to the bed, a clock in the distance struck three.

I gazed at the wizened white face of the man lying in the bed with tubes in his nose. My dad was only sixty but this man looked ten years older. I wondered, *How had he aged that quickly without my noticing? What happened to the fighter I once knew?* I touched the frail hand lying on the white coverlet. I could barely feel his pulse. Only the "beep-beep" of a heart monitor near his bedside broke the eerie silence.

Suddenly I felt a hot tear trickle down my cheek. If only I had told him the things I had been meaning to tell him over the past few years: how much I loved him; how I loved those times when, as a small child, I would sit on his knee and listen to nursery rhymes; how, as a teenager, I had appreciated his help in solving those unsolvable math problems. Now I realized I might not get the opportunity.

I lifted his hand to my cheek. It felt cool against my hot skin. "Dear God," I prayed, "give me the chance to say all the things I've been meaning to say but never found the time." I let go of Dad's hand and dropped into a chair near the bed. For the next couple of hours, I stared at his face, half expecting him to open his eyes and be my old dad once again.

Eventually Nurse Sutton, the day nurse, crept in, her soft-soled white shoes squeaking on the polished floor. She inspected the chart, took my dad's pulse, wrote the information on the chart, and left the room. By six o'clock my dad had not shown any signs of waking. I began to panic. *What if he never wakes up? What if I never get a chance to speak to him again?*

"Are you all right?" said a soft, feminine voice at my side. I turned and saw a China-doll face, with wisps of hair the color of sunflowers tucked under a white cap. She was dressed in a white uniform like Nurse Sutton but without a name tag.

"Beg your pardon?" I said.

"I heard you crying. Can I help?"

"It's been three hours and my dad hasn't awakened. I don't think he wants to fight," I said. "It's not like him. He was always a fighter."

"He's resting before the big fight," she said. Then she walked to the bed. Her long fingers curled around my dad's wrist as she glanced at her watch. Minutes later a smile crossed her cherry lips. "That's better." She released his wrist.

"The big fight?" I asked, somewhat confused by her comment.

"He's been through a lot. When he wakes up, he'll feel bad. You'll have to help him. You must show him he's got a lot more living to do."

I nodded. There certainly was a lot more living to do. I turned to thank her, but the room was empty. I hurried to the door and peered out. There was no one in sight. I returned to my chair, making a mental note to thank her when she returned.

Thirty minutes later Dr. Luther appeared and checked the chart. He looked at my dad and at the monitor. "Good, his color is coming back and his heartbeat is getting stronger."

"So he's going to be all right?"

"We'll wait and see," Dr. Luther responded. "I'll send the nurse in to check his pulse."

"But the nurse was just in," I said.

Dr. Luther scratched his head. "Funny, there's only one note recorded on the chart."

Just then Nurse Sutton entered. "I've come to take Mr. Riley's pulse."

"Don't you mean record the pulse you took a few minutes ago?" Dr. Luther asked.

"But doctor," I interrupted, "I meant the other nurse."

Dr. Luther smiled at me. "Mrs. Riley, I think you need some rest. Nurse Sutton is the only day nurse assigned to the case and the night nurse doesn't come on for hours."

Just then my dad's eyes fluttered open and focused on my face. "Where's that nurse?" he whispered. "The one with the touch of an angel?" He smiled and closed his eyes. The only sound was the "beep-beep" of the heart monitor as he slept.

by Rosemarie Riley

Rosemarie Riley is a published author originally from Australia. She has had many poems, articles and stories published for both children and adults. She attended college and taught elementary school until she moved to California with her husband and two sons. Five years ago she decided to become a writer, attending classes on writing. She can be reached at 847 Embree Crescent, Westfield, NJ 07090; Phone: (908) 928-0866; e-mail: janjriley@yahoo.com.

THE DEEP END by Matt Matteo

Reprinted by permission of Matt Matteo.

Believing in Miracles

We were all looking forward to Easter. My husband, Charlie, had run to get last minute candy for the Easter baskets. Finishing breakfast, both of our children were running and laughing through the living room. Suddenly, Ken ran into the den where I was on the phone.

"Steph is acting really funny," he said.

"Yes, I know son. I hear you laughing."

"No," he insisted, "There *is* something wrong."

I hung up the phone and walked quickly into the bedroom where Stephanie was lying on the floor, unconscious, with a small amount of foam in the corners of her mouth. Unable to waken her, I asked Ken to call 911 while I quickly assessed her condition. Though breathing, with a steady pulse, she appeared ashen.

The ambulance arrived and took her to Children's Hospital. Shortly after entering the emergency room, she began to convulse. Within minutes she stopped breathing. As the staff feverishly worked on her, Charlie arrived. We stood together, looking through the ER windows, not believing what was happening.

The doctor pulled us aside and told us he had no explanation for Stephanie's condition, but was very concerned, as her status had changed so quickly. After routine questions regarding overall health status, history and access to poisons, Stephanie was transported for a CAT scan. We prayed. In a state of shock, I could not believe how rapidly our lives had been turned upside down. An hour ago, we were eagerly looking forward to Easter and now our world was crumbling down around us.

With no remarkable results from the CAT scan, Stephanie was transported to ICU and placed on a ventilator. She lay in a coma while we sat by her side, around the clock. Expert after expert examined her, ran tests and then let us know they didn't know what was wrong with our daughter. While I hoped and prayed for answers, I was also relieved as they ruled out one serious explanation at a time. I knew that, in spite of the uncertainties, no diagnosis was good news.

After five days with little improvement, her primary nurse sat down with me at the bedside. She must have sensed my despair. "The secret at this point is to focus on any improvement, no matter how small. Ask yourself the question, is she better today than yesterday. Is she better now than an hour ago?"

"What do you mean?" I asked.

"Focus on the little things. Did she move her foot today? Is her color better? Is she trying to breathe on her own? Each hour that goes by, and she is stable, is good news. Each small improvement means progress in the right direction."

I took the nurse's advice. I stopped focusing on the darkness of the situation and started to watch for encouraging signs. Later that day, I noticed that Stephanie was trying to take breaths on her own and was "fighting" the respirator. The sixth day, I observed her moving her feet and hands. By the morning of the seventh day, she was breathing on her own and was removed from the ventilator, although she had not regained consciousness.

That afternoon, I was washing Stephanie's face when suddenly she put her arm around my neck and said my name. I thought I was dreaming and just stood there, staring at her. When she spoke again, I knew that she would be okay.

It took Stephanie a full year to recover. The doctors decided she had viral encephalitis. We helped her learn how to walk, ride her bike and read again. Against all odds, she recovered fully. We focused on small improvements each day.

I realize now that the nurse in ICU gave us the most precious gift—hope. She gave us a focus to our prayers.

Today, Stephanie is an honor roll student in high school and a member of the varsity swim team. I call it a miracle. Einstein says there are two ways to look at the world, "Either everything is a miracle or nothing is a miracle." I know a miracle when I see one.

by Barbara Bartlein

(Author's Note: A special thank you to Stephanie Brosky for demonstrating a special courage and sharing her story.)

Barbara Bartlein, RN, MSW, President of Great Lakes Consulting Group, is a motivational speaker, consultant and author. She writes "Success Matters," a popular column on personal and professional growth. She can be reached at: 2019 E. Estes Street, Suite 200, Milwaukee, WI 53207; Telephone: (888) 747-9953; e-mail: Barb@BarbaraBartlein.com; Web site: http://www.successmatters.org.

This Is Holy Ground

It was a listless, October day in the prison yard. The long, Indian Summer provided unseasonably mild weather, with no sign of winter. Prisoners at Lexington Correctional Center strolled the yard aimlessly, but every man had a plan for the future. In spite of their travails, the men were positive about getting out someday, even the "long-timers."

In the medical unit it was different. In the last few weeks there had been five deaths. The darkened, silent rooms and hallways were glum. Sadness seeped through the unit like a dense fog. It settled on the floors like a poison. Nothing seemed to disturb it. Here there was no hope. This was the end of the road. There were no plans being discussed.

The loss of friends had a telling effect on the inmates. They all wore stiff upper lips to hide their fear, but each one was alerted to the fact that there would soon be more deaths. This is where Fred was taken.

Fred was fifty-something and a handsome brute of a man. A weight-lifter from his youth, he continued to keep his body in good shape. He could hardly believe it when he found out he was seriously ill. He had shaggy, brown hair that just covered his ears. His eyes were a baby blue, so unusual looking that women looked twice; something he played to the limit.

It was the suddenness of it all that hit Fred so strongly and so wrenchingly. He had not been feeling well for months but he had been able to put it out of his mind each day. The fainting became the tell-tale circumstance that wouldn't go away.

Some quick tests at Medical, and he was on his way to the State Hospital in Oklahoma City. He was seriously ill. The doctor leaned over him, so as not to share the message with anyone else. He said, "Fred, you have Leukemia. Do you understand what this means?"

With frightened words, Fred asked if he was going to die. The doctor answered, "Maybe. I'd say you have less than a five percent chance to survive more than even a few months." He went on to say chemotherapy and brain radiation would be used in his treatment. "But I can't give you any guarantees. You will lose your hair in the radiation," he added. This bothered Fred even more.

As treatment progressed, he lost control of many of his thoughts and actions. There were long periods of unconsciousness, falling and memory loss. Fred also lost his faith. He had the desire to end it all. Surely, he thought, death could not be as bad as this.

Everything remained about the same for months. Late one night, a nurse, with the prettiest smile he had ever seen, came into his room. She asked, "Fred, would you like me to read to you from the Bible?"

This was at the height of his suffering, at a time when he suspected he was dying, or that he may even have already died. He sobbed, "Yes . . . yes, please do it now."

The nurse pulled a chair close to his bed and began. "The Lord is my shepherd. I shall not want. He maketh me to lie down in green pastures. He leadeth me beside the still waters. He restoreth my soul." She read through the long night.

From the first words, Fred let go easily and relaxed for the first time in months. A feeling of comfort, love and care swept over him. He knew that he was healing and, without any question, he had been touched by the Lord. Although he later looked for her and inquired about her, he was never able to find that nurse again. It was as if she no longer existed.

Even though Fred felt better, the doctors told him he should not be optimistic. "Very few have recovered from this type of Leukemia so far." Soon, Fred was moved to the hospital at Lexington where they took men to die. They told him nothing else could be done. The thought of his own mortality never left him.

One day, he received a letter from an old friend. A prayer handkerchief was enclosed. This cloth had been passed through the church congregation and was fervently prayed over. From that moment on, he carried the handkerchief with him and even slept with it under his pillow.

The following Wednesday was dark and rainy, with extremely loud bursts of thunder and reports of tornadoes in the area. The storm seemed to be directly above the hospital, adding to the depressing atmosphere of the medical ward.

Fred was strolling the hallway when the head nurse suddenly appeared. The stout woman held him by the shoulders and stared into his eyes as the thunder continued. She said, "Fred, you *are* going to die . . . *someday*. But I'm here to tell you it won't be as soon as you expected, and it won't be from Leukemia. You're disease is in complete remission." Only two days earlier his condition remained unchanged. Fred looked at the nurse in disbelief as she smiled and repeated the news. "You are in remission, Fred."

Fred's faith was restored. He believes the nurse who read the Bible to him and the doctors and nurses working to treat his Leukemia were all messengers of God. They came into his life at just the right time. As Fred has often said, "I know I was healed by God's holy angels."

by Rexford Moore

Rexford Moore is a geologist who explores for minerals. He graduated from the University of Oklahoma with a BS in Geology, and is a successful free-lance writer. He can be reached at 200 North Harvey Avenue, Suite 320, Oklahoma City, OK 73102-0260.

Reprinted by permission of Rexford Moore. Copyright ©1998 Rexford Moore.

[*EDITOR'S NOTE:* For information contact the **Leukemia & Lymphoma Society,** 1311 Mamaroneck Avenue, 3rd Floor, White Plains, NY 10605; Telephone: (800 955-4LSA (Voice: Toll-free); (914) 949-5213 (Voice); Fax: (914) 949-6691; Web site: http://www.leukemia-lymphoma.org.]

Never Lose Hope

I have encountered many cancer patients during my nursing career, but Tony was like no other. He was a seventy-four-year-old gentleman who had been in relatively good health until the onset of overwhelming fatigue and complaints of "just not feeling right."

After a visit to his doctor, followed by a referral to a urologist, he went through a battery of tests. They confirmed the most feared diagnosis–bladder cancer with muscle invasion. He was facing treatment options of chemotherapy followed by radiation, and extensive surgery if these treatments failed.

Tony, a World War II veteran, was in the midst of planning a long awaited trip to Normandy to attend the fiftieth anniversary of the "D-Day" celebration. Less than three months away, the trip now seemed almost impossible.

An aggressive chemotherapeutic protocol was initiated, using four potent medications. Throughout several weeks of these medication cycles he developed side effects, which required hospitalization. He was discharged with only three-and-a-half weeks remaining before his scheduled departure for France. Tony would always respond with, "I'm going, no matter what."

His focus was on gaining weight and increasing his strength and endurance. Overcoming all obstacles, Tony began his solo journey to Normandy–one suitcase filled with dressings and supplies for the chest wound sustained from chemotherapy, and the other with personal items. His family was very concerned and worried, yet grateful he gained the strength to fulfill his dream.

While in France, he was surrounded by many World War II heroes. In my eyes, he too was a hero. He was fighting the battle of his life–cancer. His determination, perseverance and deep religious faith enabled him to meet a goal that many thought, at times, was unattainable, including me. Despite the cancer diagnosis, and the many adverse effects he endured, he never gave up.

Then one day, another cancer patient asked to see me. As I

entered Ray's room, he was watching the "D-Day" ceremonies. While I prepared to sit and talk with him, I glanced up at the television. The camera briefly focused on a veteran in the audience. I was shocked. You see, this hero was my father.

How ironic that, among the thousands present that day, the camera focused on my dad. Tears of gratitude streamed down my face as I thanked Ray.

I never fully realized the impact that a diagnosis of cancer could have on a patient and the family until I found myself overcome with hopelessness, anger and despair. Even my faith was waning. Thanks to Ray, my faith and hope were renewed.

Although the future is uncertain, I find strength and hope in knowing my father will always have memories of fulfilling his dream. His faith gives him the strength and courage to endure whatever lies ahead. He taught me to never lose hope.

by Louise Fleming

Louise Fleming MSN, RN, CWOCN, completed her Masters in nursing at Anna Maria College, Paxton, Massachusetts. She is a graduate of Albany Medical Center Wound Ostomy and Continence Nursing Education program, and is a certified Ostomy, Wound and Continence Nurse. "A special cancer patient has shown me the meaning of hope." She can be reached at St. Elizabeth's Medical Center of Boston, 736 Cambridge Street, Boston, MA 02135; Telephone (617) 789-2218, or (508) 655-5853; Fax: (617) 789-2216.

God's Little Angel

She gave her life to God so many years ago.
People first rejected her, of course they could not know.

She was sent by God to do this special chore.
To go into the slums of Calcutta and help the sick and poor.

She preached of hope and helping, and loving one another.
To start with family first, our sisters and our brothers.

To open up our hearts and show the world we care.
To give our hearts to God and talk with Him in prayer.

She comforted dying beggars in her arms, and told them of God's love.
Their suffering would soon be over; their Savior waits for them above.

She lived among the beggars, the hopeless and the poor.
But knowing she was serving God, made her spirit soar.

She traveled all around the world, to help the hungry, sick and poor.
And with God's help and her willing heart, she gave them so much more.

This precious, tiny nun, who loved the people so,
Is finally with God; it was time for her to go.

They put her body on display for all the world to see.
This tiny saint, that the Lord sent, to teach God's love to you and me.

by Gail Kuhlman

Gail Kuhlman lost her mother at age thirteen. She keeps a spiritual diary and writes poems with spiritual focus to thank God for walking beside her and protecting her. "While sick with ovarian cancer in 1991, I put complete faith and trust in Him. Nurses do care; they give love, comfort and hope." She can be reached at 206 East Orlando Avenue, Murray Estates, Oceanview, DE 19970; Telephone: (302) 537-5863; e-mail: COOLKUHL@aol.com.

A Gift from Above

In the final analysis, the questions of why bad things happen to good people transmutes itself into some very different questions, no longer asking why something happened, but asking how we will respond, what we intend to do now that it happened.
~ Rabbi Harold S. Kushner

Why do bad things happen to good people? This question has been asked by many patients and caregivers. Why should any of us working in the healthcare profession be any different?

Tragedy is an all too familiar experience in the hospital setting. Whether caused by sudden death, suicide, advanced cancer in a young mother or the death of a child, no one can prevent tragedy. No one is exempt.

During the past five years, I have grappled with the meaning of suffering. As a Family Support Nurse, I have had countless opportunities to witness the effects of suffering on the lives of the many patients, families and caregivers to whom I have been privileged to minister. I believe that deep inside each one of us lies a dormant power that can redeem tragedy. Donna's story is a perfect example of this power.

During the past three and a half years I had come to know Donna, a Medical ICU nurse. She was an excellent nurse and cared deeply for her patients, as well as their families. There was one obstacle that Donna and I had discussed. She couldn't understand why patients had to endure such great suffering, only to die.

This same conversation transpired on numerous occasions until one day, when my answer came. "You are here to promote healing no matter where the experience takes you," I said. "What decision will you make to best serve yourself and those you serve? Do these decisions promote personal growth? Are they the most loving decisions for all concerned?"

The day finally came when I was certain that Donna knew in

her heart exactly what I had told her. With the enthusiasm of a child, she approached me and stated, "Joanne, Joanne, the most wonderful thing happened to me this weekend." She spoke with the enthusiasm of a lottery winner.

"I helped Mrs. Powell to die." Donna went on to explain that Mrs. Powell had battled lung cancer for many painful months. She was told she needed mechanical support to sustain her life.

Donna approached Mrs. Powell and together they openly discussed the options. Mrs. Powell was tired and didn't want further life-sustaining treatment. After careful discussion, she requested that Donna call her family. One by one her children and grandchildren gathered around the bedside. Her husband of sixty years remained with her.

As each child approached the bedside they were instructed to sit down. She spoke to each one individually, sharing her final thoughts and her decision not to prolong her life. Each child tearfully embraced her, expressing their love and acceptance. After the last grandchild arrived, about 8 p.m., the family gathered close to the bedside to pray.

After praying, the family dispersed and Mrs. Powell soon died in her husband's arms. Her husband expressed his love and gratitude for Donna's kind and compassionate care by making the comment, "I now consider you as one of my daughters." Donna left the hospital that evening feeling privileged to have been invited to share the intimacy of that moment. Perhaps that was Mrs. Powell's goodbye gift to her.

Despite the harshness of tragedy there is the triumphant hope that even the dying process can be gracious and dignified. Caring for others is a gift from above.

by Joanne Turnier

Joanne Turnier, RN, is coordinator of a Family Support Service, at Nassau County Medical Center in East Meadow, New York, which provides emotional care and bereavement support. She has redeveloped the Perinatal Bereavement Program. Both services provide on-going support during the crisis, as well as follow-up care. "This story is among many which have made an indelible mark on my heart." She can be reached at Nassau County Medical Center, 2201 Hempstead Turnpike East Meadow, NY 11554; Telephone: (516) 572-5624.

Last Dance

Children are often our greatest teachers. For one thing, they are much less conscious of human limitations and think most anything is possible. Such was the case of a small, nameless, little girl in a restaurant who empowered a terminally ill, wheelchair-bound octogenarian to rise above her limitations and to have a child-like faith that all things are possible.

Recently, five of our hospice patients were given an opportunity to maximize the pleasures of a balmy spring day. We all knew this would be the last spring for these dear souls. A church van was pressed into service and five youth group members volunteered to help make a memorable last outing possible for these patients.

The patients were loaded, with their nurses, wheelchairs, oxygen tanks and other medical paraphernalia, into this chariot and taken on an expedition to a nearby mall where, for a short while, they could forget about the hard work of dying. Chances are the squealing, happy voices of kids still resounded in that van from prior expeditions and added to the merciful forgetfulness of these patients' difficult circumstances.

I remember how it was, as a child, to be confined in a hospital bed for weeks with a severe case of mononucleosis. I recall my utter entrancement with the ordinary world outside of my sickroom on that delicious day when I was released from the hospital.

My hospital bed and its torments were soon forgotten. For our hospice patients, darkened rooms and hushed, uncertain voices were left behind and exchanged for a vast, bright, colorful world of fountains, trees, chattering families, delicious aromas and endless possibilities in that mall.

This world included the fine, tasty southern vittles of Aunt Sue's restaurant. If you have ever been through a spell of hospital food, then you know how important this was. After a grand luncheon, the patients wanted to listen to an organist playing dance music out on the patio and eat two large scoops of rich ice cream

GA

without a thought to the amount of cholesterol or fat grams they contained; and so they did.

One of these fragile, life-loving patients, Catherine, a former dancer, was wheel-chair bound on continuous oxygen therapy. Once a soul has experienced dance, it is never content with the sidelines and is forever a dancer. Her body had long since betrayed her. It had been years since she had been whisked about a ballroom floor wearing a shimmering gown.

She knew it was now or never. It was time for the last dance. She asked our volunteer coordinator, Charlene, if she could dance with her. Charlene pondered how one gets a fragile, terminally-ill patient out of a wheelchair, up on her feet and then dancing, without stumbling over her oxygen tubing. Catherine was somehow able to cling to Charlene, and they danced just a bit, right there, submitting to the limitations of her oxygen tubing. Then, exhausted, she sat down in her wheelchair.

Charlene was a very outgoing, social soul and was visiting with the other patients and staff on the patio following this small miracle— a greater one was soon to follow. After some minutes, Charlene looked up to see that Ms. Catherine had taken off her oxygen, arisen from her wheelchair, and was now dancing in the middle of the floor with a small child. This youth had not yet been taught about the limitations of terminal disease or oxygen tubes. They danced round and round that floor. Catherine returned and sat down in her wheelchair, put her oxygen back on and smiled. She died a few days later, having danced to the end.

This child had helped this departing soul fulfill a last dream. Perhaps this angel also knew that Catherine would be dancing when she experienced the magic of Heaven and would have wanted to freshen up on her dancing, just a bit, before arriving.

This dear patient's nurse was present on that dance floor and was simply astounded over the possibility that Catherine could even get up out of her chair, let alone dance; and do this without oxygen. Later on, Catherine said that was the best day she had in years.

by Craig C. Johnson

Craig C. Johnson has traveled forty nations. Having faced possible early death from a terminal neurological horror, he saw his lifetime dreams shatter. He has faced death nine times. "Life has been more than good . . . it has been truly wondrous!" Medical researcher by day, Mr. Johnson creates illusion in community theater by night. He can be reached at P.O. Box 2404, Anderson, SC 29622; e-mail: Craigjohnson15@hotmail.com.

My Johnny Angel

Make yourself familiar with the angels, and behold them
frequently in spirit; for without being seen, they are present
with you.

~ Saint Francis de Sales

At the time Johnny and I met, I had no idea that we would become angels for one another. We had met at church and started a friendship while working there together.

Following a seven year search to find spiritual happiness, Johnny became a member of our church. Our priest and choir director arranged our blind date—at a New Year's Eve party. Johnny was so handsome and such a wonderful person, I couldn't help but fall in love with him.

We had a perfect, romantic courtship and became soulmates. We shared a love together that can only be dreamed about. Five months after our first date, Johnny romantically proposed marriage at Disney World. I accepted with jubilation and we walked around the theme park wearing bride and groom mouse ears for the entire day. We were married in August in a church ceremony surrounded by all of our family and beloved friends.

We honeymooned in Disney World and knew life couldn't get any better. Three weeks after our wedding day, Johnny's health declined and he had to be hospitalized. A massive tumor was discovered. He was diagnosed with renal cell carcinoma of the right kidney with metastasis to both lungs and chest cavity. The wonderful doctor who broke the news to us held us as we cried together. To learn of such an advanced disease at the age of thirty-two seemed to be more than even the doctor could handle.

I spent that night in the chapel, crying and praying. When I arrived back in Johnny's room, he told me that he had made peace with God and was putting his life in God's hands. He was prepared to face any outcome.

"If I've been called by God, it must be because I'm needed elsewhere," he said. After praying and asking for God's guidance he finally chose his plan of treatment.

For the next thirteen months Johnny suffered through the dreadful treatments. He was hospitalized every four months, each time receiving the same encouragement to keep fighting.

Although weak and emaciated, Johnny desperately wanted to return to Disney World. We made the trip in March, with our friends. Johnny spent the day driving a scooter so he could be as independent as possible.

Johnny suffered a seizure at home, two months later. He was rushed to the hospital, went into respiratory arrest and had to be placed on a ventilator for six days. His kidneys stopped functioning which led to multi-system failures. Although the pain was excruciating, Johnny did not stop fighting. He pulled through and started renal dialysis in addition to his other treatments. He maintained his wonderful attitude and faith.

As his bone and brain tumors spread, he gradually lost his ability to communicate. That's when we discovered our own language—the language of love. Our wonderful parents stayed in shifts to care for him while I worked a full-time job. During these times of crisis our families became one. When I came home from work, we spent our evenings side by side, lovingly devoted to each other.

Johnny became unresponsive in September. Since he chose to have complete medical care when the time came, I had to abide by his wishes. He went into a full arrest in the emergency room and was brought back to life only to remain on machines. After several days he had made the decision. He had had enough and was being called home. As I held his hand and sat by his side, the doctors explained that without the machines he would not be able to breathe on his own. He would die.

Our priest stayed by our side as I held Johnny's hand. Everything was removed as he requested. We were surrounded by family and all who loved him. Slowly he said good-bye to each of us. I held Johnny's hand for the last thirty hours of his life. At one point, while our priest and I were talking with him, Johnny held up his hand and traced a tear falling from our priest's eye, and then traced a tear on my face with his finger, whispering, "No more," in a frail voice.

Crying, I looked deeply into Johnny's beautiful green eyes. I understood that he did not want any tears. He knew he was going home to be with God. During the night, I felt his grip weaken as his life faded slowly away. At 9:07 a.m., surrounded by me and our loving family, priest, friend and physician, Johnny took his last breath and was finally at peace.

I remained numb for three months and then crashed into a deep depression. As a nurse, and a strong person, I was expected to just carry on. I am still trying to find a life without my beloved husband. As I look back, I know that God arranged our meeting so I could make Johnny happy and care for him in his final days.

by Karen E. (Krishen) Ragone

Karen E. (Krishen) Ragone, RN, is a registered nurse and a 1982 Graduate of Lutheran General and Deaconess Hospitals School of Nursing in Park Ridge, Illinois. "Thank you, Dear Lord, for your love." She can be reached in Florida at: Fax: (352) 686-9878; e-mail: kragone@gate.net.

CHAPTER 6
LITTLE ANGELS

You may give them your love but not your thoughts.
For they have their own thoughts.
You may house their bodies but not their souls,
For their souls dwell in the house of tomorrow,
which you cannot visit, not even in your dreams.

~ Kahlil Gibran

Donna's Comfort

It was a hot summer day. Our baby was ten days overdue, and I desperately wanted to go to the beach. My husband, hesitant at first, eventually agreed.

"Remember to bring the bag for the hospital," I joked, confident that this would not be the day.

We had a joyous time watching our daughter, Tara, build sand castles. I felt relaxed. Being in the water brought welcome relief from the extra weight I had put on. As we left the beach that day I found renewed strength.

Within ten minutes after leaving, the pains began. They were about four minutes apart and not very intense, so I didn't share this reality with my husband. *He would only become nervous,* I thought. At home, I began to prepare dinner. I realized the pains were intensifying.

"This is the real thing!" I announced to my husband and daughter. We made arrangements for child care, arriving at the hospital after 10 p.m. The nurse started her paperwork and we walked the halls. I knew this was it. Even though Tara had been born five years earlier, the memories were still there. Several nurses assisted throughout the night, but I didn't seem to connect with any of them. I wondered if they would have time for me.

I dozed and went into a dream-like sleep. A feeling of serenity came over me. It felt as if I were asleep but the vivid image made it seem as if I were awake. There were four angels standing next to me, and one of them even looked like my friend, Debbie, who died a few years earlier. The angels seemed to take the labor pains away. When the nurse came to check on me I was definitely awake. I no longer saw the angels but peace seemed to fill the room. I knew I wasn't alone as I prepared for the journey ahead. I was ready.

As morning approached something didn't feel right. The labor wasn't progressing as the nurses thought it should. They called the doctor in and everyone looked concerned. I prayed for comfort, answers and help. I wanted to see my angels again, but I knew I wasn't alone.

My angel did arrive with the 7 a.m. shift. She introduced herself as Donna and told us she was the supervisor. It was comforting to know she was experienced. As she looked directly into my eyes, I felt reassured. There was a gentleness in her spirit. When she took my pulse, it was as if she were comforting my entire body.

Donna answered every question with assurance to calm my fear. The sparkle in her eye let me know she cared. She entered as a stranger, but provided loving care. It seemed like we had known each other for a lifetime.

The conversation between the doctor and nurse led me to believe that things weren't going well. At this point, I had been awake for the last twenty-four hours and was losing stamina. The doctor was considering a Cesarean-section while Donna was thinking of alternatives. She radiated a confident presence. The doctor treated her with respect, listening attentively.

Donna recommended techniques for visualization, breathing and positioning that eased my pain and helped my labor to progress. She offered praise when I met the challenge and never left my side. She believed that I *could* deliver a healthy baby.

For the next three hours, Donna orchestrated the many people who were preparing for a possible C-Section. She was my strength. Donna's comforting voice and gentle presence helped convince me that I really could do this. I gave birth to my son, Michael James, at 10:14 a.m. by natural childbirth.

The seriousness of what was happening to me and the possible complications that might have occurred were explained to me the next day. There were moments when I knew the doctor was alarmed. Donna helped me to believe that I could overcome the problems I faced. The angel that arrived at 7 a.m. was a blessing—one that I remember every time I see my little Michael.

by Teresa Dowe Huggins

Teresa Dowe Huggins is an educator, counselor and leadership consultant for teen programs. She inspires others to find light in the darkness and opportunity in the obstacle. She speaks to teen and adult groups, helping others believe they can make a positive difference in this world. She can be reached at 41 Williams Street, Clinton, NY 13323; Telephone: (315) 853-5064; e-mail: huggins@dreamscape.com.

The Cast-Cutter

After years of hospital nursing, I loved my new job in a busy family-practice office, performing a wide variety of duties: phlebotomy, spirometries and EKGs. I accepted each as a new challenge and mastered all of them with confidence.

Well, almost all of them. I was still nervous whenever I cut off a cast. To prove to the patients (and to me) that the motorized saw wouldn't cut their flesh, I always put my fingertip next to the spinning circular blade. I then explained how the cotton padding underneath the cast snagged the blade and stopped it before it reached the skin. But, in spite of my own reassurances, cutting casts still made me a bit nervous, especially when the patient was a squirming four-year-old boy.

Danny had broken his arm in a playground accident a few weeks earlier, and I assisted the doctor in applying his cast. When I rewarded his bravery with double trinkets from the toy chest, Danny and I became buddies. He had complete confidence in my ability to remove his cast. That made one of us.

With a reassuring smile I fired up the cast-cutter and started cutting the cast, hoping he'd think the trembling was from the vibration of the saw, not my hands. The motor buzzed and bits of plaster flew as I methodically pressed the whirling blade back and forth along the length of the cast. Danny started to fidget in the chair and his face flushed.

"Doing okay, Danny?" I asked.

"I'm okay." He smiled meekly. " It don't hurt." But his facial expression and wiggling told me something was making him uncomfortable.

Thankfully, just then, the final part of the cast was cut. I carefully pried it apart with the cast spreader. After showing him the blunt-ended scissors and promising him they couldn't cut his skin either, I began cutting the cotton padding and underlying stockinet. Danny wiggled some more and even winced a bit when I spread the cast further and gently lifted his arm out of the cast.

I gasped to see a long purple streak on his inner arm! My mind raced for a diagnosis. *Phlebitis? Necrosis? Had I cut him?* There was no blood. There, inside the opened cast, wedged between the layers and embedded in the padding, was a purple crayon. Bewildered, I looked at Danny.

He said, sheepishly, "It itched!"

by LeAnn Thieman

LeAnn Thieman is a nationally acclaimed speaker and author. A member of the National Speakers Association, LeAnn inspires audiences to balance their lives, truly live their priorities and make a difference in the world. Her book, *This Must Be My Brother*, details the Vietnam Orphan Airlift. She has written stories for seven *Chicken Soup for the Soul* books and is a co-author of *Chicken Soup for the Nurse's Soul*. She can be reached at 6600 Thompson Drive, Fort Collins, Colorado, 80526; Telephone: (877) THIEMAN (Toll-free); Web site: http://www.LeAnnThieman.com.

Just Add Water

Many people say that laughter is the best medicine. Sometimes you just need a little water. I believe that life is a collection of moments—one connected to another by an invisible thread and woven into the fabric of our minds as memories. You can recall an event at any time, and connected to it will be a string of stories. "Do you remember the time . . . ?"

When my son turned eighteen we learned that he had cancer. They said it was a rare form called Ewing's Sarcoma. The tumor, in his case, was in his lower left leg.

My son is now twenty-four and, as of his last complete checkup, he is healthier than ever. But whenever I find myself remembering those long, difficult months of chemotherapy, after the surgery, there is one person who always comes to mind—Lori, his nurse.

Lori is, in a big way, responsible for my son's recovery, but not so much because of the professional care and attention she provided. She was a professional in every sense of the word, but Lori was just a little outlandish. She loved life. In the children's cancer wing of this hospital, death was never an option when Lori was around.

Why? Water gun fights with massive, needle-less syringes. Suddenly, without notice, the battle would begin. Laughter would erupt from down the hall. Everyone would rush to their doors and slowly, cautiously stick their heads out, never knowing from what direction the attack would come.

SPLAT! SWOOSH! One young child runs from the room followed by Lori. An attack from the rear. Lori is soaked as she passes by a young girl in a wheelchair who had been waiting since dinner time for the big event.

"Oh no! Not you!" Lori cries out. "Where did you get that?" she asks of her young, rolling attacker.

"My mom got it for me," she says, laughing so hard she was nearly in tears.

A miniature super-soaker. Lori surrenders. These moments

didn't last very long. The laughter and its wonderful healing powers last a lifetime.

The first night I stayed with my son was his first night to receive his treatments. I was devastated. I excused myself from the room as they finished connecting "Red Death" to his intravenous. That was just one of the nicknames for the various chemicals being poured into my son's veins.

Lori came rushing down the hall to the sitting room where I was. "I was wondering when this would hit you. It always happens right after the first injection," she said.

I couldn't even speak. I sobbed. She held me until I stopped. Then she sent for one of the other parents. One of the experienced ones who had been down this road.

"Take care of him. You know how he feels," said Lori.

Then suddenly, out of the deep, dark feelings of despair, I heard laughter once again, in Room 723. The battle returns. The war against fear. The war against giving up. The fight for life.

Before my son had completed his treatments, I asked Lori how she could be so upbeat and full of fun. She said, "In any given situation we always have choices. Our mission, our goal, is to save lives. The fact is, we lose some along the way. Whatever the outcome for my kids, I want to make sure they never stop being kids. I will not permit this disease to kill their right to be a child."

In that moment, I came to realize that if a person walks across my property without me knowing it, except for footprints, there is little or no evidence to prove they were ever here. Lori, the nurse, danced across our hearts and left an impression that will last a lifetime.

I have since revisited that floor looking for Lori. I am sorry to say that she had been dismissed. It had something to do with laughter, love and a little water. You can still see the water, but unfortunately, it is in the form of tears shed by her absence.

by Bob Perks

Bob Perks is a Professional Speaker, and author of *The Flight of a Lifetime!* He is a member of the National Speakers Association, National Writer's Association, International Platform Association and Optimist International. He can be reached at 88 North Pioneer Avenue, Shavertown, PA 18708; Telephone: (570) 696-2581; Fax: (570) 696-1310; e-mail: Bob@bobperks.com; Web site: http://www.bobperks.com.

[*EDITOR'S NOTE*: For information on Ewing's Sarcoma, as well as other types of cancer, contact the **American Cancer Society**, Telephone: (800) ACS-2345; Web site: http://www.cancer.org.]

THE DEEP END by Matt Matteo

Reprinted by permission of Matt Matteo.

My Beautiful Children

My children do not have eyes of blue, sparkling with merriment. Instead, they are soft gray, brown and green and stare at the world, unseeing. They are special children because they are blind.

My beautiful children do not laugh at the joyous sounds of music or marvel at the sound of a bird singing. They are special children because they are deaf.

My beautiful children do not run or dance. All their limbs are turned and twisted. They are in wheelchairs almost every day of their lives. They are special children because they are spastic.

My special children cannot hold a favorite toy. Their brain wins the battle over their bodies when any movement is attempted. They will always need someone to take care of them.

My special children will never read or hold a job. They are brain damaged.

My special children cannot blow bubbles into the air. A respirator is needed every minute of the day to keep them alive. Their chest muscles do not receive messages from their brain to breathe.

My beautiful children cannot do many things, but they have the ability to love, and it's impossible to resist loving them in return.

I take care of these beautiful children. I am their nurse!

by Victoria Molinari

Victoria Molinari, RN, a practicing nurse for more than thirty-two years, is a member of the Nurse's Standard and Review Board of the Board of Education of New York City, the New York State School Nurses Association and the National School Nurse Association. "I have cared for many beautiful children. I realize the courage they put forth in their struggle to survive." She can be reached at 2165 Victory Boulevard, Staten Island, NY 10314; Telephone: (718) 698-3110.

A Special Little Angel

When you let the love of a child transform your heart, you are renewed.

~ Judy Ford (*Wonderful Ways to Love a Child*)

The morning of April 19 finally arrived. It was to be a very special day but, as the morning sun came through my window, I greeted the daylight with mixed emotions. Samantha, our four-month-old daughter, was to be baptized. She was to have two sets of god-parents, a decision that came quite easily for my husband, Tom, and me. We didn't have to worry about which family members to ask. Without hesitation we chose our good friends, Barb and Al, and a very special woman named Kathy.

Tom and I bonded very closely to Kathy. It wasn't your typical co-worker or college roommate type of bond; it was more than that. Kathy was a nurse in the Neonatal Intensive Care Unit (NICU) at Children's Hospital of St. Paul, in Minnesota. We met her in December 1996, when our son, Benjamin, was in the hospital. He was born three months too early and only weighed one pound eight ounces. He had many health problems and endured six surgeries during his seven and a half weeks in the hospital.

One Saturday evening, Tom and I decided to go to mass at a local church close to the hospital. Although we weren't regular members of this church, our sense of faith became much stronger with little Ben in the hospital. We recognized a nurse from the NICU, who sat just across the aisle from us. She attended mass with her family and afterwards introduced herself as Kathy. We had a short conversation with her before proceeding back to the hospital to visit Ben.

Several days later we saw Kathy in the unit. We asked her about her church and told her we were thinking about becoming members. Benjamin was getting much worse and Kathy could see the newborn joy draining from our faces. She asked us if she could invite her congregation to pray for Ben. We were both honored that this woman, who didn't even know us that well, was doing this for us.

Christmas was just around the corner and Benjamin was taking a turn for the worse. We prayed that God would show us the sign that it was time to let our little son go. It was the morning of December 19. Tom and I had spent the last two days and nights in a small room at the hospital. We woke up with our arms around each other and knew we had to let Benjamin go; he was suffering.

When we walked into the NICU we were in a daze. There was constant activity going on around us but I felt as if I were going in slow motion. Benjamin's daytime nurse, Sally, took one glance at us and knew by the look on our faces what the day would bring. Then Kathy walked over to us and gently placed her hand on mine. She said, "I will be taking care of little Ben today." Kathy had only taken care of Ben once before.

We had made the most difficult decision in the world—to discontinue life support for our newborn son. To give us some privacy, the nurses moved Ben and all his equipment into a separate room, just for us. This was the first time we were allowed to be alone with our tiny son.

Kathy was with us for the next seven hours. We talked, we hugged Ben, we kissed him, we gave him a bath, we changed his clothes, we combed his hair, we took pictures, we prayed, and we hugged him and kissed him again. We did all the things we were supposed to be doing with a healthy baby seven and a half weeks ago. Now it was time to turn his ventilator off. Kathy made sure we were comfortable and then left us alone.

We held our tiny son for the last time and cried. Kathy entered the room periodically, kneeled beside us, touched us and said nothing. Her quiet presence was comforting.

On Thursday afternoon, December 19, 1996, Benjamin passed away. We asked Kathy if she would like to say something at Ben's memorial service. She hesitated at first but, on the day of the service she delivered a touching eulogy that was spoken from the heart, in honor of Ben.

We have stayed in touch with Kathy ever since. About a month after Samantha was born, I invited Kathy over for lunch. She sat on the couch, holding and admiring our baby daughter. We hadn't talked much about Benjamin's last day, but I had to ask her a burning question.

"Kathy, what kind of training did you have, to be able to take us through the stages of death like you did, so compassionately?"

She looked at me for a few moments, and with a soft voice responded, "I didn't have special training for that. I was guided by God."

It was clear that Kathy was going to be Samantha's godmother, and a part of our lives forever. Samantha's baptism was very special, not only was she baptized that day, but we had the presence of a special little angel named Ben.

by Deborah Ann Rhody

Deborah Ann Rhody is an active board member for The Spare Key Foundation, a local non-profit organization that offers both financial and emotional assistance to families of critically-ill children. Deborah also works part-time and lives in Inver Grove Heights, Minnesota with her husband, Tom, and daughter, Samantha. She can be reached at e-mail: tdrhody@uswest.net.

[*EDITOR'S NOTE*: For information contact: **The Spare Key Foundation**, P.O. Box 612, South St. Paul, MN 55075; Web site: http://www.sparekey.com.]

Fairy Godmother

We are like children, who stand in need of masters to enlighten us and direct us; and God has provided for this, by appointing his angels to be our teachers and guides.

— Saint Thomas Aquinas

I have been transformed, helped and astounded by the many nurses I am grateful to have known during the course of my baby, Maggie's, long illness. I could write a separate story about each one, describing how good they have been to me and my family.

JoAnne, a pediatric home care nurse, came to our family in January of 1996, when Maggie was thirteen-months-old. She got to see Maggie at her best, during that six week stretch of time when she was at home—healthy, growing and laughing.

After seven surgeries over the course of the year, I was tired of all the medical-support people traipsing in and out of our house. Though I needed and relied on them, I also resented their presence. I wanted some privacy and wished I could care for Maggie and her twin sister, Elizabeth, all by myself.

At times I may have been less than gracious, even downright hostile, but JoAnne never took it personally. She accepted Maggie and Elizabeth into her extended family of "adopted grandchildren," bringing lots of love and attention, along with a special book or toy, each week.

By mid-February, Maggie's heart was failing and she had to return to the hospital. JoAnne came over on her days off from work to baby-sit Elizabeth, so I could be with Maggie. While I received the priceless gift of time with Maggie, Elizabeth experienced firsthand the wonder of a grandmother's love. She began calling JoAnne "Nana" and eagerly anticipated her visits.

Maggie became sicker and her cardiac problems could not be managed by medication or additional surgery. She was put on the waiting list for a heart transplant. In April we got the news. A new heart was waiting for her in Pennsylvania. I was on my way to the hospital when the call came. My husband, Bob, met me there.

We sat with Maggie, excitedly watching the flurry of activity going on around her. We were thrilled. This was her chance for a "normal" life. I looked forward to the time she would come home with us for good.

For ten days after the transplant, JoAnne and Gail, our neighbor, who was also a pediatric nurse, juggled their schedules so they could watch Elizabeth.

We were stunned when the doctors could not get Maggie off of the life support machines. Each day, we watched our dreams for her gradually disappear, as machines did the work of her heart and lungs. She was tough, and had been through so much, we assumed she would get through the transplant too. But her little body finally gave out after a long week and a half. At three in the morning we made the last trip home without her.

JoAnne, and my best friend, Lisa, were there for us, helping with the details of daily life that grew overwhelming in light of baby Maggie's death. JoAnne became my friend, my therapist and the mother I wished for, during those bleak days and months after Maggie died. She got me through some of the worst times of my life, visiting every week.

JoAnne is a permanent fixture in our lives these days. I remain astounded by her selflessness. She became Elizabeth's godmother, and knowing her has brought us all a little closer to God.

by Rebecca Parant

Rebecca Parant, RN, is the mother of Elizabeth and Daniel. She currently works in a geriatric long term care facility. "I enjoy my work and am probably more compassionate because of my experiences as the mother of a critically ill child." She can be reached at 23 Houghton Street, Barrington, RI 02806.

Angel on the Spot

When you are grateful you are rich.
~ Sir John Templeton

"Mr. Cassidy, before you leave, the doctor needs to speak with you." The nurse's words were disturbing. It was 1:30 a.m., and I had just kissed my wife, Grace, goodbye. She was totally exhausted after hours of intense labor with significant blood loss. I naively assumed there was some minor difficulty, perhaps something related to my wife's rare blood type.

Grace sat up slowly and with the look of great concern uttered, "Let me know what the doctor says."

As we walked toward the neonatal unit, the doctor spoke gently. "Mr. Cassidy, your baby has had a problem."

I felt sick–the dreadful feeling you get when life takes an abrupt turn for the worse. "Is Christopher okay?"

"Your baby had trouble breathing and went into cardiac arrest. The intensive care nurse happened to be in the nursery and noticed Christopher was turning blue. She gave your baby CPR immediately. He's breathing well now, but we had to place him in intensive care. We'll have to conduct some tests to determine the cause."

"How long did Christopher stop breathing? Will he have any brain damage? I thought he had a great *APGAR score," I blurted out.

The doctor motioned calmly toward a woman in rose-colored scrubs. "Mr. Cassidy, this is Shari, the nurse who administered CPR to Christopher."

Only hours earlier, when Christopher first went to the nursery, I had seen this same nurse wrapping him in his little green blanket. She even wheeled him over to the window so that his grandparents could take a longer, loving look.

She reassured me. "Mr. Cassidy, I was right there when your son turned blue. I gave him mouth-to-mouth resuscitation and chest compressions immediately. He turned pink right away. His heart rate is still low, but it's much better than it was."

I later discovered that Shari normally worked in the intermediate intensive care nursery, but since no babies were admitted there that night, she came over to the regular nursery to help out. Over the next several months, my wife and I spent many restless nights wondering whether our son would be all right.

Today, Christopher is the most beautiful, loving child in the world. Shari has a son named Christopher, too; and amazingly enough, he also went into cardiac arrest shortly after birth and was saved by a nurse.

Several months ago, as I was listening to a speaker address a group of healthcare recruiters in Chicago, it struck me. He said that it is very important to take the opportunity to express our gratitude in life. You only get so many chances. Well, this is my chance and I'm not going to pass it up. Shari, thank you for saving our son.

by Christopher M. Cassidy

(**APGAR Score**: *A method of assessing the overall physical condition of a newborn based on heart rate, respiration, muscle tone, skin color and response to stimuli.*)

Christopher M. Cassidy is a proud father and Director of Information Systems at *Nursing Spectrum* (Web site: http://www.nursingspectrum.com). He can be reached at 8324 Kay Court, Annandale, VA 22003; Telephone: (703) 849-0760; e-mail: ccassidy@NursingSpectrum.com.

A Child's Understanding

It was hard to tell just how much Jeannie understood about her sister's condition. There was so much sadness in her eyes each time she visited. They were, after all, best buddies–the oldest barely fourteen and the youngest only five years old.

It was as if she had already lost her big sister. Suzanne could no longer play Candyland with her, or dance to the song, "Honey, Sugar, Sugar." But they drew pictures together for awhile, until the drugs took effect, and Suzanne finally drifted off. Jeannie was reluctant to leave her sister; she always straightened the covers and kissed her tenderly when she had to go.

As a curious five-year-old, Jeannie had many questions for Rosemarie, Suzanne's primary nurse. Rosemarie allowed Jeannie to be her "helper" while caring for her patient. Jeannie would hand the nurse the unopened dressing supplies and bed linens, and then position the call bell and phone so her sister could reach them. She seemed to sense that this person cared for Suzanne, and she wanted to be a part of that too.

When it became evident that the end was near, our entire family attended group therapy sessions at the hospital. Rosemarie was always there to answer any of the clinical questions. While the other siblings seemed to understand the dying process, as much as one can, Jeannie seemed to need the most comforting, which she sought from Rosemarie.

I think Jeannie saw Rosemarie as someone who helped her sister, and perhaps Jeannie felt that she could help her sister too. Her main concerns were about the place called "heaven" and how she could visit her sister there.

Rosemarie discussed her concerns with me. She explained that Jeannie was too young to understand the finality of death. One day soon, she would need our help because death was coming.

"How will I know when she understands?" I asked.

"She will let you know," was her reply.

GA

Suzanne died in April, and Rosemarie attended the funeral. Jeannie was unusually quiet and never left Rosemarie's side.

"She's confused," Rosemarie quietly explained. "She sees sadness and tears all around her. She doesn't yet feel the pain of her loss, but she will in time."

"How will I know when she realizes her sister is gone?" I asked.

"She'll let you know, in her own way."

The subsequent days turned into months and although the grieving continued, life was somewhat normal. However, there was something that concerned me deeply. Jeannie still talked about her sister in the present tense, as if she were still with us.

On one occasion, someone who was unaware of our tragedy asked Jeannie if she had any brothers or sisters. As I held my breath, Jeannie, without the slightest hesitation, responded, "Yes . . . my big sister, Suzanne."

When I later asked Rosemarie about this incident, her response was, "This is normal and to be expected."

It was a few months after Jeannie's sixth birthday, and a few days after Christmas, when I heard the sobs coming from Jeannie's room. I heard talking, but I knew she was alone. As I walked into the room, I found her crying into her pillow, holding her newest Christmas treasure, a Barbie® Doll, high over her head and into the air.

"What is it?" I asked.

"Mommy, I lied," Jeannie cried, as tears stained her cheeks.

"You lied?"

"Yes, I lied to God." She said, looking toward the ceiling.

"About what?"

"I tried to trick Him. Grandma said that if I prayed every night, God and Suzanne would hear me. So I held up my new doll for Suzanne to see, then I asked God if Suzanne could reach down and hold her. I only said that because, when she put out her hand, I was going to pull her down from heaven, with all my might, so she could stay here and be with me again. I think she has to stay there Mommy . . . but why?" Then she began crying again, as I joined her.

Our salty tears saturated the pillow as we held onto each other for a long time. We were all in the healing process together. Rosemarie's words of wisdom rang true. Jeannie had finally felt the reality of her sister's death, and her healing had just begun.

by Gerry Bernard Sheridan

Gerry Bernard Sheridan, RN is a Public Health Nurse employed by the Visiting Nurse Association of Long Island, New York. She can be reached at 2193 Clover Court, East Meadow, NY 11554; Telephone: (516) 483-1581.

An Angel in Disguise

I still remember that May night as though it were today. I was twenty-eight weeks pregnant and still coping with the shock of being told that my baby girl's heartbeat had stopped and labor would have to be induced. From the time my husband and I had found out I was pregnant, we had been looking forward to the birth of our first baby.

How could it be that it was going to end this way? I had taken my prenatal vitamins, eaten the right foods and had just seen my midwife the week before. Everything had been going as a normal pregnancy should. What could I have done wrong? All of these thoughts were floating through my head as I awaited the birth of my baby.

Being a nurse myself, one would think that my nursing instincts would come into play and put my mind at ease. Just as I thought that nothing could prepare me for being on the other end of caregiving, Sue came in and introduced herself as my nurse. Like me, she had also gone through the loss of a baby inutero, only her loss occurred at thirty-eight weeks.

Sue shared her own personal experience with me. She explained some of the things I would be feeling and going through. Sue also reassured me that I did not cause this to happen, and I was not to blame myself. "Sometimes things happen and you just don't know why." I took all of what she said to heart. Although it was tragic to hear Sue's story, at the same time, it comforted me. I realized that I was not alone in experiencing the loss of my baby.

As the night went on and my labor pains became more intense, Sue continued to provide me with support. On one occasion, I remember her saying that she hoped I would have my baby on her shift.

On May 30, 1998, at 4:20 a.m., little Amber Nicole was born. Sue was by my side the whole time. Right after Amber was born, Sue took her for pictures, footprints and handprints, and a lock of hair to be snipped for a momento. She even contacted the clergyman to baptize our baby.

My husband and I were able to spend time alone with Amber. It broke my heart to see my husband, with tears in his eyes, holding our lifeless baby daughter in his arms. Even though Amber was stillborn, nothing could ever replace the joy and pain I felt deep within my heart when I gave birth to her and held her close.

Two days later Amber Nicole was laid to rest. Since Amber's birth, family and friends have planted trees and made donations in her honor. My husband and I have also planted a rose bush in her memory.

As quickly as this ordeal began, it ended physically. The mental anguish of losing Amber, although not as intense today, will always remain. I don't think I could have gotten through that night with anyone else as my nurse. Sue could relate to everything I was going through. She had lived it herself.

I firmly believe things happen for a specific reason. I may never know exactly why Amber died, from a medical standpoint, but I do know there was a reason; just like there was a reason why Sue and I were in the same place at the same time. My baby, Amber Nicole, will never be forgotten, nor will "Nurse Sue," who showed me that angels do exist and life does go on.

by Karen St. Andre'

Karen St. Andre', RN, is a nurse in the telemetry and medical intermediate care units at the University of Maryland Medical System. "The opportunity to share my story not only gives me the chance to express my thankfulness to the nurse who cared for me, but also provides a source for healing." She can be reached at 1518 Carriage Hill Drive, Westminster, MD 21157; e-mail: karengoa@aol.com.

The King

My son, Ryan, the most wonderful boy a mother could ever want, suffered from a childhood cancer. For almost two years he went through intense chemotherapy. As if that wasn't enough, he had five major operations in an attempt to remove the tumor; and sadly, none of them worked.

After each surgery Ryan would wake up and ask, "Mom, did they get my tumor?" And each time I had to be the bearer of bad news and say, "No, Ryan, they didn't. I'm so sorry!" Then we would cry. As I think about it now, it is still a heart-breaking ordeal.

My "angels of mercy" were remarkable. I called them that because, without a doubt, they were "angels." I cried and laughed with them, and even became best of friends with some of them. They shared some of the most monumental moments of my life and will remain in my heart forever.

Until the last three months of Ryan's life, I was hoping for a miracle. There had to be a miracle that could save his life; that could cure his cancer. I spent every day prepared for battle, ready to fend off anyone with a negative attitude. I was committed to allowing only positive vibes.

Ryan's nurses loved him. He was always so willing to let them help him, and he seldom complained about anything they had to do. Ryan knew his nurses were the greatest.

I remember, not long before he died, someone asked him if he had a wish. Without hesitation he responded, "Yes I do." When they asked what it was, Ryan quickly answered, "I wish I could win $50,000 so I could give it to all my nurses, and to all the nurses in the world." Ryan knew what they meant to him. He knew he was receiving the best care in the world.

The nurses would often come to visit him when they had a day off. Sometimes they would even call me from home; some still do. I can't count the number of times I laughed and cried with them. I knew we had made friendships that would last a lifetime.

At night, when Ryan was asleep, gathering around the desk became a social event for me. We shared many discussions on Ryan's care, and what the next move would be. I had complete trust in them. The staff would even allow me to take part in ordering food, the highlight of the night. After three months I felt like this was my second home.

It took slightly more than two weeks for Ryan to pass. Those were truly the worst days of my life. I thank God for the nurses who knew me so well, sometimes better than I knew myself. They knew what to say, when to say it and when not to say anything at all.

Right up until the end. Ryan did things his way, as usual. Just before he died he said, "Hey, all you guys. I'm not growing up, I'm going up. Get it? Ha! Ha! Look at me. I'm Fly'n' Ryan!" He passed into his new life on Sunday, October 25, 1998 at 5:55 p.m.

All the nurses had asked to be called; a hotline had already been set up for this purpose. The list seemed endless and included people from all over the hospital. One by one they each stopped to say goodbye to their buddy, Ryan, better known as "The King." Each one came from different walks of life but, when it came to Ryan's care, there were no differences. They all cared in their own special way.

Letting go is so hard, but I know I must. I love all the caring nurses, the "angels of mercy" who looked after Ryan. I will remember you forever. Go now to the other children who await your loving care and compassion.

by Elizabeth Weyhknecht

Elizabeth Weyhknecht has worked as a waitress, restaurant manager, hospital housekeeper, patient service associate and patient care associate. Ryan's Web site, http://www.geocities.com/heartland/Oaks/3058, gives part of Ryan's story, and includes a tribute to his nurses and doctors. Elizabeth can be reached at 317 Bath Avenue, Apt 30, Long Branch, NJ 07740; Telephone: (732) 229-4168; e-mail: ElizabethW99@webtv.net.

"V" Is for Victory

Most of us envision healing as an illness transformed into a healthy state by medical means. Nurses are an integral part of this process. Most nurses have the innate gift of assisting in the healing process through their compassion, love and desire to help others to "get well." Nurses give medications, provide comfort and safety, promote rest and act as advocate for their patients.

As a nurse, I can honestly say that we do what we do best—including all those "nurse" things, like a smile, gentle touch and understanding. It makes both patient and nurse feel good, and plays a large part in the patient's recovery. This is what makes us nurses.

Sometimes patients die despite our heartfelt efforts. We find this difficult because death is looked at as the failure to heal and is contradictory to our "purpose" as nurses. This is the time when "healing" must truly come from our hearts. Sometimes the healing must *begin* with dying. For the nurse, the most challenging venture of all is becoming part of the process of dying.

Death is an affirmation of our own mortality. This is the time when we must look within, to see our deepest selves, to examine who we really are and our own beliefs and values. This is when healing comes solely from our loving hearts, a special time in our nursing career when we dare to be our real selves. We dare to allow ourselves to feel the love, the hurt and the pain. We become vulnerable and cry because we care.

As a nurse and mother, I have comforted many children and have seen too many of them die. I go home at night, hug my own children, and lie awake remembering the perpetual pain of those bereaved parents. My memories eventually fade until the next time.

One of these memories is that of Ryan, a child who only lived to see his eighth birthday, having been diagnosed with cancer at six-and-a-half. Despite his brief life, Ryan lived a *full* life. He taught everyone around him the meaning of love. He had a message to

GA

spread and a limited time in which to do it, and in the end he succeeded.

He had an unusual passion for the letter "V," his peace sign usually reserved for photo sessions. After his death, we realized that his "V" was really a symbol for *victory*. It was *victory* that, in the end, brought his family together; his sign for triumph by teaching us about love.

At first, Ryan seemed like a typical oncology patient. His family was trying to cope and his mother refused to believe in anything short of a miracle. She had great faith and over the years painted a beautiful picture of heaven for her son. He was unafraid.

Many of us were convinced that if a miracle were to take place this certainly had to be it. We prayed that if medicine couldn't heal Ryan then maybe God could. But as time went on his condition worsened. He spent the last three months of his life on the pediatrics unit.

During that time, the nurses spent countless hours comforting Ryan's mother. At first, death wasn't an option in her mind. It was during those last few weeks of her son's life that the "doorway" to healing started to open. When she was ready, we slowly "opened that door" and stepped through it together. Day by day she came to accept the inevitable. We gave her our hearts and our love, and together we cried.

We did experience a miracle. The healing miracle we all waited for was the effect that Ryan's illness and death had on those around him. His illness brought a family back together, helped the staff attain a higher level of camaraderie, involved other members of the community, brought three religious leaders together and touched the hearts of everyone.

A magical thing happened at Ryan's other home–pediatrics. The healing power of love was magnetic; it filled Ryan's room and seemed to attract everyone. There was music, children dancing, tears, storytelling, hugging, laughter and visitors. In the center of it all was Ryan, who loved it and never missed a moment. That was what he wanted, healing with love. He wanted everyone to feel it in their hearts and to begin their healing while he was busy dying.

We used to call him "the little man" because he seemed to speak prophetically. Ryan once said, "My guardian angel, Alex, sits on the foot of my bed. He told me I am free. I don't have cancer anymore."

As Ryan's mother said, "Ryan's 'V' was for victory over the cancer that took his life. It set him free to start his new life in heaven. My 'V' for victory was when I allowed myself the courage to let him go."

Victory was ours for the taking because we knew where Ryan was going. That "V" was made from two arms held high–one from Ryan, the other from his family, friends and nurses. Although the healing still continues, I know it began with the love we gave from our hearts.

by Debra L. Skelly

Debra L. Skelly, RN, BSN, CPN, has been a registered nurse for nineteen years. After graduating from Seton Hall University, where she earned a BSN degree, she became a nationally Certified Pediatric Nurse. She enjoys her work on a Pediatric Unit at Monmouth Medical Center in Long Branch, New Jersey. She can be reached at 8 Wealthy Avenue, Middletown, NJ 07748; Telephone: (732) 495-5433; e-mail: Hera8301@aol.com.

[*EDITOR'S NOTE*: For grief support after the death of a child, contact **The Compassionate Friends, Inc.**, a national nonprofit, self-help support organization which offers friendship and understanding to families who are grieving the death of a child of any age, from any cause. P.O. Box 3696, Oak Brook, IL 60522-3696; Telephone: (630) 990-0010, or Toll Free (877) 969-0010; Fax:(630)990-0246; Website:http://www.compassionatefriends.org]

Training of the Heart

*Your vision will become clear only when you can look into your
own heart. Who looks outside, dreams; who looks inside awakes.*
                                                        ~ Carl Jung

It was a cold, gloomy November afternoon. I was a nursing student assigned to pediatrics. I helped to admit Jason, a three-year-
old boy who had been physically abused by a member of his family. This poor child had been kicked repeatedly with a steel-toed
boot and was barely conscious. Today I can still see the fear in his
eyes. I spent that afternoon just holding him, trying to comfort
him, in what was surely a terrifying situation.

As the social worker discussed his case with me, she mentioned
feeling uneasy about a recent visit she had made to the boy's home.
"Except for his mother's stuffed animal, that Jason wasn't allowed
to touch, there were no other toys to be found. There was no food
in the house except for a half loaf of moldy bread, but there were
plenty of street drugs lying out in the open," she said.

I also discovered, during our conversation, that the police officers
who brought Jason in were very concerned, and would probably
be stopping by to check on him later. I didn't see them during my
shift, but I wanted desperately to talk with them. As I reviewed
Jason's chart, I realized this was his third birthday; some "happy
birthday."

That evening, feeling extremely upset that anyone would do
such a thing to their own child, I went to visit my parents. My
brother, Scott, came in as I was wrapping a birthday gift for the
child. Scott told me about a very disturbing case that he had worked
on that day.

My brother, a police cadet for a local police department, carried
a battered little boy on his lap, all the way to the hospital. Scott

said, "Jason was so bruised and weak he could hardly speak. He was so skinny. God knows when he ate last."

As he told me this, I realized this was the same child that I had cared for that day. So my husband, brother and I put together a birthday party for Jason. I baked a cake and we bought him presents; something he'd never had—his own toys.

Later that evening, when we returned to the hospital, it appeared that some of the nurses had the same idea. Each of them had gone down to the gift shop to buy birthday gifts for Jason. One nurse even made a big "Happy Birthday" sign to hang over his bed. We gave him quite a party and, although he seemed to love it, we were well aware that no one from his own family was there for him.

Although I wanted desperately to be a foster parent for Jason, the social worker told me that he would most likely be placed with his parents again; and that is exactly what happened. Jason was placed with the very people that hurt him.

I would like to tell you this story had a happy ending, and that Jason eventually led a happy life, but tragically he never had the chance. Eight months after he was returned to his family, he was brought in to the emergency room—dead on arrival. I can only pray that the party we gave this young boy brought him some momentary happiness.

Children don't deserve the abuse and humiliation they sometimes endure at the hands of those who are supposed to love them. That day, I received my training of the heart. Jason made a difference in my life and he will always hold a special place in my heart.

by Cindy Wilhite

Cindy Wilhite, RN, is a registered nurse, specializing in perinatal nursing. She lives in California with her husband and four children. Her favorite pastime is reading a good book, but she also loves to fish and cross-stitch. She can be reached at 1502 Glenwood Lane, Bishop, CA 93514; e-mail: cinderk@gte.net.

[*EDITOR'S NOTE:* For information contact the **National Foundation for Abused and Neglected Children (NFANC)**, a nonprofit tax-exempt organization dedicated to the prevention of child abuse and neglect. Other activities include improving the administration of juvenile justice in America. P.O. Box 608134, Chicago, IL 60660 e-mail: nfanc@hotmail.com; Web site: http://www.gangfreekids.org.]

Bobby

I will never forget the twelve-year-old boy who taught me the real meaning of nursing. Bobby and I met during my senior year at Peter Bent Brigham Hospital. We were allowed to spend six weeks in any specialty of our choice. I chose the Leukemia/Tumor Therapy Division because it was meaningful, and I hoped to work there after graduation.

My very first assignment was to care for Bobby, who was dying of a malignant brain tumor and had already had one eye removed. Within a few days, he became my case study. No one, including me, understood how he remained alive.

Bobby was a very bright and alert boy, in spite of pain and a growing tumor; but he never lost his sense of humor. He had a younger brother, and his parents lived in a nearby town. During the next six weeks on the unit, I never met Bobby's father, and his mother visited only on rare occasions. Bobby couldn't understand why his mother visited so infrequently. I later found out that she was afraid her younger child would "catch cancer" if she visited Bobby.

Over the next few weeks, I became very close to Bobby. There was such a strong bond between us that I even visited on my days off. He loved to have someone read to him at bedtime. I got to know the *Lone Ranger* books by heart.

At 2 a.m. one Tuesday morning, I got a call asking if I would come to the unit immediately. Bobby wasn't doing well and was slipping into a coma. He wasn't expected to live through the night. His parents had been called, but they couldn't get there until about 9 a.m. Bobby asked the nurses if they would summon me.

When I got there he wanted me to read to him and hold his hand. After a short time he said, "Would you pretend that you're my mom? I love you." It was the least I could do for him. I loved him too, but it wasn't easy. He closed his eye, and at 6:30 a.m. he just stopped breathing, still holding my hand.

Bobby wasn't my son. Although I hadn't given birth to him, we shared something special during those six weeks. When I look back now, over forty years later, I know that Bobby gave me more than I ever gave him.

Nursing involves alleviating not only the physical pain but also the emotional pain that can be devastating. Coping with this can be a monumental task. As nurses, we must consider all aspects of illness.

I married and had two daughters and five grandchildren. Because I love my profession, I have always continued to work as a nurse. Bobby taught me the greatest lesson early in my career. He cared enough for me to let me into his life for only a brief time. How privileged I was to have known him.

by Anonymous

The author is a practicing registered nurse who prefers to remain unnamed. She is a graduate nurse of 1955 and has no plans to retire. She is currently employed in a maternity department at her local hospital. "Nursing is the most rewarding profession I can imagine."

[*EDITOR'S NOTE:* For information contact **The Pediatric Oncology Branch of the National Cancer Institute**, which is part of the National Institutes of Health (NIH). They provide patients, families and physicians with an overview of the type of treatments available for children with cancer, and of the research conducted by investigators at the Pediatric Oncology Branch. Building 10, Room 13N240, Bethesda, MD 20892; Telephone: (301) 402-0696; Web site: http://www-dcs.nci.nih.gov/pedonc/Index.html.]

CHAPTER 7
UNTIL WE MEET AGAIN

When you were born, you cried and the world rejoiced.
Live your life in a manner so that when you die the world
cries and you rejoice.

~ Native American Proverb

When CPR and ICU Were New

"You mean, you can bring someone back to life after they're dead?" I asked with skepticism. After graduating from nursing school in 1961, I worked at Presbyterian Hospital in Philadelphia. At that time, my roommate was also working there in one of the first ICUs in the country. One day, she came home to tell me about a new technique to save lives called CPR.

"Yes, back to life," she beamed, and a description of the procedure tumbled from her lips. I listened to every detail and decided right then and there I would try it at my next opportunity.

I had agreed to take on some occasional private duty nursing assignments at the hospital. One night, a few weeks later, I went in to work on the 11-7 shift. I was to take care of an elderly lady, Mrs. Moore. Around 2 a.m. she went into cardiac arrest. I yelled for help, but there were no code teams in those days. I rolled her bed down and prayed I could remember the verbal instructions my roommate had given me.

I started CPR by compressing her chest, not knowing how much pressure to exert, while alternately breathing into her mouth. I concentrated on the ratio of compressions to breathing as I watched her body for any sign of movement. My heart was pounding and adrenaline was flowing through my body. Truthfully, I didn't expect any reaction. Only in the Bible did miracles occur, and I didn't feel like any miracle worker.

Mrs. Moore started to cough and opened her eyes to look at me. She was alive. What an unbelievable feeling that was. I had brought someone back to life. I was in awe and gave thanks to God.

Around 6 a.m. that same morning, the patient in the other bed arrested. Convinced of my invincibility by then, I tried to resuscitate her, but to no avail. I felt somewhat defeated but was still thankful for the miracle that had already happened.

I went home at 7 a.m. but could hardly sleep that day. I just wanted to relive the events. I was to go back on duty again with Mrs. Moore at 3 p.m., but before I could get dressed, I received a phone call. A nurse from the hospital called to inform me my patient had died "again," and I was not to come in. I felt like a balloon that had been punctured. My miracle seemed to have evaporated, and I questioned the reason I had ever been able to revive her the first time.

Later, I went back to the hospital and mentioned to a fellow nurse how deflated and confused I felt. "What's the use of doing CPR and saving a life if the person is only going to die again?" I asked.

"Oh, Lois, it wasn't in vain," she explained. "The morning after you performed CPR and brought Mrs. Moore back to life, she had the opportunity to see her son one more time. He had just arrived from Florida and hadn't seen her in years. He was able to share those last precious hours of his mother's life with her." And then I knew why God provided this miracle.

by Lois M. Studte

Lois M. Studte, RN, retired after working thirty-six years in the health field, the last twenty-six in a community college. She lives in Milford, Delaware, is married with three children and two grandchildren, and reaches out to the community through her involvement on committees, boards and commissions. She can be reached at 1004 Dogwood Avenue, Woods Haven, Milford, DE 19963; Telephone (302) 422-9385; Fax: (302) 422-2161; e-mail: Lstudte@dmv.com.

GA

A Couple Doses of Laughter

A cheerful heart does good, like medicine.
~ Proverbs 17:22a (The Living Bible)

Hospice was on the scene, and the family was on alert. "Take a week off from work *now*," my friend urged, "and enjoy your mom while you can. I saved my vacation days and never got a chance to use them. You'll never regret it." My boss agreed, and those final three weeks of Mom's life were the best times of reminiscing we'd had in years.

"It's funny what you remember at times like these," Mom said. "Like that beatnik joke you got so tickled about in junior high."

"What beatnik joke?" I asked. "How did it go?"

"It went something like this: A pedestrian had been hit by a speeding car in New York City and nobody seemed to care. He was lying in the gutter, bleeding and crying out, 'Help me—somebody help me.' People rushed past, ignoring the injured man. At last, a beatnik shuffled up and stood there looking down at him, wide-eyed. The man was encouraged by a compassionate face. 'Please,' he begged. 'Call me an ambulance.' The understanding beatnik nodded and said, 'Man . . . you're an ambulance.'"

Although we never needed to call an ambulance for Mom, we found that the hospice nurse who was assigned to her had the heart of an angel. Nurse Cathy came regularly to the house to monitor Mom's records and medications. Mom responded well to the matter-of-fact way Cathy handled awkward subjects like bodily functions. One day, as our pleasantly efficient nurse was logging in statistics with pen poised over the chart, she asked the standard question, "How are your bowel movements?"

"Not much," said Mom.

"Not much?" She raised her eyebrow. "Are you having

discomfort? Loose stools? How would you describe what you mean by 'not much'?"

"Just a lot of rootie-toot-tootin' going on." She smiled and winked.

Lighthearted. That was Mom. Nurse Cathy was still shaking her head and chuckling when she left the house that afternoon. Things got mighty serious toward the end, but Mom's wit and sense of humor never dimmed.

"Are you okay, Harriet? Do you need help?" Dad asked anxiously one morning. Mom was leaning forward with her head down and her hands on her knees. She was trying to coax her body from the edge of the bed into a wheelchair. Talking was difficult. She just couldn't get enough oxygen into her lungs. Nurse Cathy and I stood by, ready to lend a helping hand. Concern deepened in Dad's voice. "Harriet, are you okay?"

She couldn't answer. Instead, she gave a half smile, curled her right hand into a ball and hung a universal "thumbs up" sign in the air. For a fleeting moment there, Mom looked like "The Fonz." Our laughter made her chuckle with us, and it was all the momentum she needed to get from the bed to the chair.

Truly, God has built remarkable coping mechanisms into human beings. Not only did He give us the capacity for faith, but a funny bone to lessen the pain of hurting places where medicine can't reach.

Dear Lord, thank you for angels of mercy, like hospice nurses, and for the emotional safety-valve of humor.

by Candy Abbott

Candy Abbott is a speaker, Bible study leader, founder of Delmarva Christian Writers' Fellowship, and author of *"Fruit-Bearer"* and *"Mourning Breakers."* She and her husband, Drew, are partners in Fruit-Bearer Publishing, a desktop publishing service designed to help beginning writers get their inspirational works into print. She can be reached at P.O. Box 777, Georgetown, DE 19947; Telephone:(302) 856-6649; (302) 856-5422 (W); e-mail: Dabbott@dmv.com.

[*EDITOR'S NOTE*: **The Hospice Foundation of America** assists those who cope either personally or professionally with terminal illness, death and the process of grief. For information contact: 2001 S St. NW Suite 300, Washington DC 20009; Telephone: (800) 854-3402; Fax: (202) 638-5312; or, 777 17th St. #401, Miami Beach FL 33139; (305) 538-9272; Fax: (305) 538-0092; Web site: http://www.hospicefoundation.org; e-mail: Hfa@hospicefoundation.org]

Please and Thank You

Speak to me softly,
  and caress my skin gently.
For although I am dying,
  I am yet still alive.

I am still rather young,
  not yet even my grandparents' age,
But here I lie in this hospital,
  in this room all alone.

I know this is hard for you,
  because you tried to give me hope.
But for all that I have suffered,
  I am ready to die.

I have lived a full life,
  full of smiles and love.
I would like to die as I have lived,
  surrounded by my family and friends . . .
Full of dignity and pride.

So please, as I lay here,
  helpless and unresponsive,
Remember I was once like you,
  young, healthy and invulnerable.

So please,
  speak to me softly.
And caress my skin gently,
  I am yet still alive.

by Ann Rossander Turner

Ann Rossander Turner, RN grew up in Wilmington, Delaware and graduated from the University of Delaware College of Nursing in 1988. "I wrote this poem while working as a registered nurse on an oncology ward." Presently, she stays at home with her children and teaches part-time. She can be reached at 302 Green Hill Drive, Anderson, SC 29621; Telephone: (864) 225-9340.

Lunch Dates

Mother was delighted when I became a nurse. A long time ago she had dreams of becoming a nurse too, but that was before marriage and children. We enjoyed spending precious time together on our "lunch dates" after I was married and had two children of my own. The time we had together meant more than simply sharing a meal. Being together was a cherished gift–a gift we gave to one another– a gift we enjoyed as time allowed. The word *time* is short and simple–and often taken for granted. We shared our hearts and souls during our uninterrupted moments in *time*.

My life was hectic and occasionally chaotic. There never seemed to be enough time to juggle everything that had to done. Keeping all of the balls in the air at the same time was an almost impossible task. Still somehow, Mother and I always managed to make the time to have our special "lunch dates."

I'll never forget one particular afternoon in early April. The two of us drove to the mall for a morning of shopping before we "did lunch." After walking for only a few minutes, she pointed toward a display of brilliantly colored spring dresses. "Let's stop in here," she said in a child-like voice filled with delight. This was an unusual day because Mother seldom indulged in the luxury of spending money on herself.

We walked over to the finery, and she eagerly shuffled through the hangers. After scrutinizing each dress, she finally pulled one out and held it up with an inquisitive glance. "Look at this beautiful blue one," Mother exclaimed. "Is there enough time for me to try this on dear?"

Without a moment's hesitation I said, "Certainly. After you have it on come out and model it for me." Mother was a generous size, and it was wonderful to see her rare excitement over a new dress.

She appeared from behind the fitting room curtains and slowly sauntered toward the full-length mirror, turning around and around

ɢA

to view every angle. She looked at me with the wide-eyed enthusiasm of a schoolgirl.

"Where could I wear this if I did buy it?" she inquired. "A graduation or . . . a funeral?" I was thinking ahead to our son's college graduation in May. We both agreed that would be the perfect opportunity for her to wear the new dress.

As we walked out of the store mother tried to disguise her discomfort. I noticed she was walking more slowly than on previous outings, and she was breathing harder with each new step. She stopped frequently to window shop and discuss the displays, but I knew in my heart that she was trying to disguise her need to catch a breath. When I mentioned it, she dismissed the subject with her usual, "I'm just fine dear . . . not used to walking in these gosh darned sandals."

We seemed to be closer than ever. We shared feelings and thoughts about everything and everyone in our lives. Suddenly I saw her in a different light. We surpassed mother and daughter. We were close friends–two adult women, connecting.

Two weeks later, on a lovely Sunday afternoon in April, my father telephoned me at home, hysterically mumbling something about paramedics. He instructed me to meet him at the emergency room, as quickly as I could.

I drove to the hospital, trying to concentrate on the traffic, despite trembling hands and a racing heart. I gripped the steering wheel for support. This was the hospital where I worked, and my car seemed to pilot itself.

The emergency room nurse was waiting for me at the door. She immediately escorted me into a tiny, dimly lit office. There sat my father, shaking and sobbing. He stood up as I walked over to him. We hugged. His tear-filled eyes disclosed the dreadful truth. He managed to choke out a few words. "She never knew what happened. Her heart just stopped. I did all I could for her but . . ." Then he fell into my arms, and we both cried.

It seemed like a nightmare–so unreal. The soft-spoken nurse gave us a few details about mother's condition and assured us that death had come quickly. Then she took us to see Mom, leaving the three of us alone for our final farewells. Before the nurse left the room, she said gently, "Take as long as you need," closing the door behind her.

Mother was lying so peacefully on the stretcher, covered almost entirely by a white sheet, except for her pale face and shoulders. Although I had seen many deceased patients before, this was different. This was my one and only Mother, and my first experience with losing a dear loved one. Dad and I held onto one another as we cried.

That shopping trip suddenly seemed like ages before. Thank God I had the chance to get to know and appreciate my mother while she was still alive. Not everyone has this miraculous opportunity.

The funeral director requested that we bring mother's burial clothing with us the next day, and we would finalize the arrangements. When Dad and I stepped into her closet, the first piece of clothing we saw was her new blue dress, with the tags still dangling from the sleeve. I choked back the tears as I remembered her recent question, "Where could I wear this if I bought it?"

Holding up the dress, I said, "I know mother would want to wear this one." Dad looked up with tear-stained cheeks and nodded in agreement.

Mother looked beautiful at the viewing. Her blue dress went well with her pale complexion and soft pink cheeks. I will always be grateful to this generous, caring woman who gave me life, her time and unconditional love.

by Laura Lagana, RN

Society's Forgotten Child

They brought her in on a stretcher–a cold, inanimate object supporting her frail, time-worn body. Gently moving her to a slightly more comfortable bed, I noted that she didn't move a muscle. Even her eyelids remained in their half-opened, half-closed position. Her breathing, erratic and stertorous, filled my ears, and a knowledge of impending death clicked somewhere in my mind. Her blood pressure was dangerously low and her pulse, which could be counted by the throbbing pulsations in her throat, was slow. I knew from experience she wouldn't last long, and at age ninety-two, nothing more than comfort measures would be administered.

The physical assessment completed, I began to look at her as an individual–a person–someone who had more than her present time to account for in this life. My heart ached for the lifeless form before me. She weighed no more than seventy pounds. Every bone was prominent, especially her facial architecture. Her cheek bones jutted out inches from the orbits of her eyes, and a perfect outline of her skull could be differentiated. She could have been used as a demonstration piece in any basic anatomy class for skeletal structure except for the arthritis which had settled in her joints, making movement difficult, if not impossible. On her head, a few wisps of perfectly white hair lay like flaccid appendages of her soul.

I opened her eyes. They had lost their color and brightness. I wondered what she might be thinking inside, if anything. *Do comatose patients think? Is it possible? What do they discuss with themselves? How must it feel?*

I phoned the nursing home to see if there was any family who might be with her during her last moments. At least they could hold her weathered hands and tell her they loved her. Hearing is the last sense a dying person loses. A spoken word from a loved one might help her on her final journey.

There was no family nearby. A daughter and a son were flying in but would not arrive before late that evening, in time to view the body—but not the soul. I was horrified at the thought of her going through the "door of death" alone. I returned to her bedside, sat in a chair and reached for her hand. I leaned over to her ear and whispered, "I'm here, and I shall stay. I won't leave you. Don't be frightened." Two strangers brought together by circumstances beyond their control.

As I sat holding her long, spindly fingers in mine, I wondered how often her children had held them recently. So many times children grow up, become successful and find they just don't have time. Mom and Dad are shuttled to nursing homes where they can sit and reminisce, trying to outdo each other with successful children stories, until finally the day comes when they smile no more and fail to look forward to another day. Then they come to us and die.

I brushed over her cave-like eyes with a cool cloth. *Was she uncomfortable? Was she too cold? Too hot?* I fussed over the sheets and blankets and wished she could communicate with me, just a little. I returned to my seat and picked up her hand again.

How long ago was it that she had laughed at jokes and enjoyed a family picnic? How many runny little noses had she wiped or dirty little hands had she washed? How many times had she given birth and then fed those hungry little mouths? How many tears had she wiped away with her apron on a warm summer's evening?

When was it, so long ago, that she had delighted in her first kiss? What color was her whitened hair then? Had she laughed with her lover as they ran through a flower filled pasture? It was hard to imagine her as a child with a mother of her own, learning to walk and then run, eating mud-pies, selling lemonade, playing with friends, her first date and perhaps a quick wedding day before her new husband went off to war. So much life in a lifetime, but no way to share it now. I prayed that good memories were with her now.

Her eyes opened momentarily and captured mine. I squeezed her hand and smiled. Hopefully, she thought I was her daughter. In the next moment her eyes closed in death. The eyes which had once sparkled with the recognition of friends, with love's first intimate encounter, with the joy of a newborn child and, with the miracle of life itself, accepted death.

Her soul began the journey into eternity. I quietly arose, acknowledged the time of her demise and covered her. Society's forgotten child breathed no more.

by Pat Clutter

Pat Clutter RN, MED, CEN is "Nurse-At-Large" living in Strafford, Missouri. She maintains a variety of positions: emergency nursing and house supervisor at a large trauma center in Springfield, Missouri; teacher at a local community college; writer and editor for publishing companies; a cruise-ship line nurse on board; and occasional flight nurse for a medical fixed wing service. She can be reached at 9361 East Farm Road 112, Strafford, MO 65757; e-mail: clutter@dialnet.net.

Death Is not Always Failure

I know for certain that we never lose the people we love, even to death.

~ Dr. Leo Buscaglia

A twenty-eight-year-old cancer patient taught me a very important lesson. Cherry fought her disease for seven years with chemotherapy, bone marrow transplants and experimental treatments. Now there was no hope. She was terminal, and we were using comfort measures only.

The last time Cherry spoke to me she asked, "Are you okay?" I replied, "No." The sadness in my eyes at her impending death gave me away. She reached out to comfort me and said it was going to be all right, she was fine. After thanking me for my concern she closed her eyes.

Although she was thin and weak, her eyes were still full of life. Her brothers, sister-in-laws and mother were all at her bedside. Everyone was cheerful, laughing and talking, but giving physical support too: ice chips, sips, backrubs and turning. She was still completely responsive. Then her mother sent everyone away and fell asleep in a chair next to her daughter's bed.

When Cherry's breathing began to slow, I awakened her mother. She held and stroked her daughter's hands, telling her she loved her. As she watched her daughter take one last breath, I stood quietly by her side, saying a silent prayer for her and the family. As I stepped from the room in search of another nurse to assist me, I felt uplifted.

There have been many times in nursing when I have felt intensely overwhelmed and disheartened with death, especially when I have been unable to save the "young one's." A strong sense of guilt and failure stays with me for weeks.

This time the guilt was lifted from my heart. Cherry let me off the hook. I did help her. I did comfort her and her family. She taught me a valuable lesson—death is not always failure.

by Pamela J. Brown

Pamela J. Brown, RN, has been a nurse since 1975. Her nursing experiences include medical-surgical, high risk nursery, obstetrics and delivery. Her goals are to obtain a bachelor's degree and to publish a book. She has been working at Valley Lutheran Hospital, Mesa, Arizona, since 1990. She can be reached at 1720 W. Isleta Ave, Mesa, Arizona, 85202; Telephone: (Work) (981) 4455, ext. 480.

Those Wonderful Angels of Mercy

In December 1997, a patient on our medical unit captured the hearts of every nurse who cared for him. Although Mr. Day was gravely ill, he was kind, thoughtful and appreciative to staff and fellow patients. In conversations with him, he talked about past memories, good and bad. As he reviewed his life, counting the many blessings he had, he was sad. His life was coming to a close, but he had put life into perspective. While still with us, Mr. Day wrote this poem.

Philomena Camputaro

Those Wonderful Angels of Mercy

When at first you arrive,
Perhaps barely alive,
Through the door
You can see them peeping.

When you're sick and so weak,
And its comfort you seek,
They come to your side
To cheer you and keep you from weeping.

They come uninvited at night,
To make sure you're all right.
Then they wake you,
To see if you're sleeping.

But their kindness shows through,
By their interest in you.
And they make you feel safe
In their keeping.

You cannot deride,
For they work with much pride.
Those wonderful ones,
My nurses.

by Roy E. Day (Deceased)
Suggested by Philomena Camputaro

Roy E. Day passed away on Feb. 28, 1998. Mrs. Day says of her husband, "Roy was a man that never met a stranger. Everyone he met became his friend."

Philomena Camputaro, RN, is a nurse at Yale New Haven Hospital. "Mr. Day touched our hearts deeply, as so few in life do." She can be reached at 15 Oberlin Road, Hamden, CT 06514; Telephone (203) 397-1361; e-mail: Philssony@aol.com.

This Is the Calling for Me

The gem cannot be polished without friction, nor man perfected without trial.

~ Confucius

I am a nurse and have been in the medical field for more than fifteen years. I love it with a passion, but it wasn't always like that.

I was nineteen and working the night shift. I was new, not only to this nursing home, but to the medical community, and not quite sure if this job was for me. It was one of my first nights. Everything was dark and quiet, much different than when I was training on days.

One of the patients had just passed away. I thought to myself, *I have to do what? Oh no!* All of a sudden I didn't like this job. This was clearly not for me. *I don't want to go into that room, into that situation!*

I was nervous and scared, though I couldn't let anyone know. *Okay, she already passed away so what do I have to be afraid of?* I took a deep breath and got through it.

Trembling, I made my way into the dark room. The curtains were drawn and the only light that could be seen was above the bed—a fluorescent lamp that gave off an eerie glow, which only added to my discomfort.

As I stepped beyond the curtain to take care of her, I was suddenly overcome by the presence of something soft and tender. A comfortable peace came over me. and I realized a presence in the upper left corner of the room. It was as if someone were there. Although I knew that no one could possibly be there, I still looked anyway.

I was then able to continue on with my original intentions but with a renewed sense of comfort and love. I said a prayer and gave thanks to God. From that point on, I realized that this was the calling for me.

by James T. Coan

James T. Coan, RN, has been in the medical field for more than fifteen years and is currently working in coronary intensive care. He can be reached at 4670 Walden Drive, Winston-Salem, NC 27106; Telephone: (336) 288-0024; e-mail: Jcoan@Hotmail.com.

Home for Christmas

A man does not always choose what his guardian angel intends.
~ Saint Thomas Aquinas

Christmas of 1998 was our first year without Mother. While she was here in spirit her physical presence was painfully absent. Years ago she was diagnosed with heart disease and the doctor suggested that we consider hospice care. We chose not to consider that option; not because hospice isn't a wonderful entitlement and service, but because of the criteria to qualify for the program.

The doctor had given mother only six months to live. Had she known this, it would have meant a certain exit for her. The family agreed that if we gave up on her she would surely give up too. Open heart surgery and congestive heart failure were but a few obstacles she had already overcome. She was sinking deeper into depression despite our efforts to elevate her spirits.

Thinking back, I realize how difficult it was to reach her and what a toll it took on the family. Things were going well when mother became extremely ill and nearly died of a serious heart infection. We even had conversations about her funeral arrangements.

After spending fifteen days in ICU she whispered, "I'm sure I won't make it through this setback." Then she tried to give me her wedding ring, but I refused, assuring her she would wear it again. At the darkest hour, mother began to make progress.

She was afraid we would think her crazy or under the influence of medication, when she told us what she had seen. During the night she had caught sight of someone standing over her shoulder, giving her the feeling of peace and letting her know she was supposed to carry on. "I saw my angel. She turned my life around," she said.

That was more than fours years ago. Her focus was no longer on dying but on living. A nurse pinned a small angel to her hospital gown and that little angel became part of her daily wardrobe. Mother soon began collecting angels. She seemed to be more at peace than ever before and enjoyed a new life, traveling and spending more quality time with family.

October of 1998 was the beginning of another decline. She developed congestive heart failure and in a matter of weeks was in and out of the hospital twice. On her last admission, she was made a code, which meant that if her heart stopped the medical staff would make every effort to resuscitate her. Mother did code and the chaplain consoled us. We braced for the worst only to be blessed with her survival once again.

Despite the pain of broken ribs, pneumonia and her weakened condition, mother laughed with us. We took turns staying with her and ate anything that would come from a vending machine.

Three days later her heart stopped. During our prayers we were notified she was breathing again. *How many more times was she to be shocked and her life prolonged?* The doctor informed us that Mother had suffered extensive cardiac damage. We unanimously decided there would be no more codes.

We went home that night with a heavy burden. Mother surprised us all and bounced back one more time. She made her final peace and had spoken to her angel. She called a few of us into her room at a time and, in no uncertain terms, said that she didn't want any tears. She wasn't afraid to die and announced her final wishes in detail. She was ready to go. We each had our turn to say what we needed to say—without tears.

We never said goodbye, only goodnight and that we loved her. Days passed as we sat vigil, until she was ready to be released to rehab for physical therapy. The thought terrified us because of the pain she had, but her spirits and sense of humor remained high. On Saturday night we all had a few laughs during our visit. My sisters bathed her on Sunday and brushed her hair. Then she phoned my father, finishing with, "Goodnight. I love you."

Mother was supposed to start physical therapy on Monday morning. We were informed that she sat on the edge of the bed and finally let go. It's so obvious now that she was being given instructions on how to properly prepare all of us for her departure, including herself.

Mother looked like an angel as she lay in her coffin. Her special pin was carefully displayed on her silk dress. While we were making the funeral arrangements, a wooden angel, that had been securely mounted to her front door for years, fell down with a loud thud. At that moment we felt peace in knowing she was finally at rest.

I had frequent dreams of Mother. It was always so vivid how she told my father to come join her. Dad later developed lung cancer and became a hospice patient himself. I lived each day with him as if it were his last. He told us that he didn't think he would be around for Christmas, although he seemed to be somewhat better. We enjoyed every day that we had together. He missed Mother and looked forward to being with her again.

My father passed away on October 29, 2000. Although Dad will never be home for Christmas again, at least he and Mother can finally celebrate–together.

by Judie Sinclair

Judie Sinclair is an author, motivational speaker and president of Positive Impact. Her goal is to motivate others to elevate their thinking and take action to improve themselves. She has both attended and assisted with Jack Canfield's Facilitating Skills Seminar, in Santa Barbara, California. She married her best friend, and is the mother of a blended family. She can be reached at 12660 Lakeland Drive, St. Joseph, MO 64506; Telephone: (816) 233-3959; e-mail: Mimisinclr@aol.com.

[*EDITOR'S NOTE:* For information contact the **American Lung Association**, 1740 Broadway NY, NY 10019; Telephone: (212) 315-8700; e-mail: info@lungusa.org; Web Site: http://www.lungusa.org.]

There Is a Reason

I had been a registered nurse for fifteen years when, one day, I received the dreadful call that no mother ever wants to receive. My son had been critically injured in a motorcycle accident.

Horrified, I raced to the hospital. Suddenly, all of my nursing professionalism and critical care experience seemed to leave me. I'd been through this with other families, but now *I* was one of *them*. Upon my arrival at the hospital, I was told that my son had not yet reached cardiac death, but that his chances of living seemed unlikely.

I stayed at my son's side for five days and nights until the doctors confirmed what I already knew in my heart to be true. My twenty-year-old son, Daku, was brain dead. Knowing my son's wishes and feelings, I knew what had to be done.

The decision to donate his organs was both the easiest and the most difficult decision I have ever made. It was easy because I knew my son wanted to "live on"–a wish that could certainly be fulfilled through the process of organ donation.

The decision was also difficult because I hated to let go. The tears from the previous five days finally stopped. I looked into the faces of Daku's two little sons, his brothers and sisters, grandmother, and other family members and friends. I knew there must be a reason for my son's untimely and tragic death. As the days went on, I came to know that reason.

Six months after Daku's death, I was recruited to work as a transplant coordinator, which involves managing potential organ donors. I also worked as an organ donation consent coordinator, counseling other grieving families and requesting consent for organ and tissue donations.

Today, I am actively involved in the transplant system. I am now acutely aware of the need for increased and more focused education. When I was approached about doing public service announcements to help promote organ donation I never hesitated for a second. But this was only part of the reason for my son's death.

As I became more involved with donor families, transplant recipients, transplant candidates and the general public, my understanding of the reason became broader. My ongoing work in the community has helped me to realize that there are many fears and concerns related to organ donation. To help address these concerns, I formed a national organization to heighten organ and tissue donor awareness, primarily in minority communities.

I encourage everyone who has ever pondered what they would do, if faced with the momentous decision to donate a loved one's organs or tissues, to dry your tears and make the decision to give the gift of life.

by Diana J. Barnes (Carter)

Diana J. Barnes (Carter), RN, BSN, is a donor mother, transplant professional and nursing instructor. Thank you: Dr. Milton Stroud, PhD., friend and mentor; mother, Julia Bryant; sister, Mary Bond; brother, Anthony Barnes; children Junie, Daku, Faraji & Rashida; National Council On Minority Education in Transplantation (COMET); Coalition on Donation; and the New York Organ Donor Network. She may be reached at P.O. Box 567, New York, NY 10027; e-mail: PHYSICALS1@aol.com; Web site: http://transweb.org/comet.

Dad

Daddy was dying a slow death from metastatic lung cancer. My sister, Carol, took him to her home in Cambridge, on Maryland's eastern shore; a nice place to be if you can't stay at your own home of many years; a nice place to be if you are dying. This wasn't Daddy's choice, but it was the best we could do under the circumstances.

Each weekend my family and I made the trip to visit with him and to give Carol some respite. During the week we kept in touch with daily phone calls. Daddy chose not to have any treatment, palliative or otherwise. His health continued to go steadily down hill.

Then one day he lapsed into unconsciousness and was taken to Dorchester General Hospital. I had to learn this painful news from my daughter. My husband and I had just returned home from a wedding.

Pack . . . gather the family . . . hurry . . . the hospital said we needed to come quickly . . . the end for Daddy was near. As night fell, we drove the hour and a half in almost total quiet. Our sorrow was exhausting. I prayed a selfish prayer that Daddy would "hold on" until we got there and we had the opportunity to be with him.

We entered the room. Daddy's large brown eyes were open, searching frantically, but not focusing on anything in particular. His size had diminished to a frail, small and helpless man. Morphine was slowly dripping into his body to ease the pain. He was monitored closely by the nurses for comfort and pain control.

He was alone in a dreary room with sparse accommodations—the room of the dying. Daddy waited for us, and I believe he knew we were there with him. My sister and I were by his side, talking softly to him—such a kind and gentle man. We were praying for a quiet passing, crying about that moment and the days to come.

We only had a few hours with Daddy before God, in His mercy, claimed him. We watched Dad take his last breath and surrender peacefully. I went from the room to tell the nurse that he had died. Two nurses came in—one listened with her stethoscope to his silent heart and the other quietly checked him with dignity and respect.

Maryland law does not allow a nurse to pronounce death, so a doctor was summoned. The other nurse was a large, male nurse who stood with us at the foot of the bed. He wrapped his big arms around me and gave me a gentle, sympathetic hug of comfort. His colossal arms encircled me as he recognized the child who had just lost her daddy.

I shall never forget his act of mercy and compassion. I knew that he truly cared. His sincere professionalism gave me a feeling of warmth, love and respect.

by M. Theresa Hommel

M. Theresa Hommel RN, BSN, is a public health nurse consultant in a local health department in Maryland. She has thirty-five years of public health experience. Her father was the mainstay of her childhood and adult life. She can be reached at 625 Maple Hill Lane, Crownsville, MD 21032; Telephone: (410) 923-6773; e-mail: Tthommel@juno.com.

ABOUT THE AUTHOR

Laura Lagana, RN, is an author, professional speaker and registered nurse who enjoys writing and speaking about real-life personal experiences, as well as healthy inspiration.

She was born in Traverse City, Michigan. Ten years later, she moved with her family to Philadelphia, and eventually to Delaware.

During her junior year in high school, her best friend persuaded her to volunteer as a candy striper at the Delaware Hospital in Wilmington. Torn between pursuing a career in nursing or journalism, she thought the hospital volunteer experience would help her to decide—and it did.

Four years later, in August 1969, she graduated from the Bryn Mawr Hospital School of Nursing in Bryn Mawr, Pennsylvania. Her nursing experiences have included medical-surgical, intensive care, rehabilitation and orthopaedics. During the last seven years of her clinical nursing career, she specialized in orthopaedics and attained orthopaedic nurse certification.

In the spring of 1997, Laura joined her husband, Tom, as a full-time partner in their own business. Together, they attended Jack Canfield's intensive, eight-day facilitation skills seminar in Santa Barbara, California, in July 1997—the catalyst that transformed both of their lives.

Due to the demands of corporate travel, Laura's husband had to spend a great deal of time on the road. After raising two sons and welcoming a grandson, she savors the privilege of working together with her mate. Today, after making a gradual transition from nursing to writing and speaking, she enjoys the best of all three worlds.

Laura is a co-author of *Chicken Soup for the Volunteer's Soul*. She is also a contributing author of *Chicken Soup for the Couple's Soul* and *Chicken Soup for the Prisoner's Soul*.

Her professional affiliations include the National Speakers Association, American Nurses Association, National Nurses in Business Association, Pennsylvania State Nurses Association, Bryn Mawr Hospital Alumnae Association and Delaware Literary Connection.

Laura can be reached at Success Solutions, P.O. Box 7816, Wilmington, DE 19803; e-mail: NurseAngel@LauraLagana.com; Web site: http://www.LauraLagana.com.

RESOURCES

Nursing

Advance for Nurses
Greater Philadelphia/Tri-State Metro Area, Merion Publications, Inc., 2900 Horizon Drive, Box 61556, King of Prussia, PA 19406-0956; Telephone: (800) 355-5627; Web site: http://www.advancefornurses.com

American Nurses Association
Web site http://www.ana.org
600 Maryland Avenue, SW, Suite 100 West, Washington, DC 20024
Telephone: (202) 651-7000; (800) 274-4ANA (4262); Fax: (202) 651-7001

Florence Nightingale Foundation and Museum
Web site: http://www.florence-nightingale-foundation.org.uk/fhistoryframe.htm

National League for Nursing
Web site: http://www.nln.org
61 Broadway, New York, NY 10006 #33rd Floor
Telephone: (212) 363-5555 or (800) 669-1656; Fax: (212) 812-0393

National Student Nurse's Association (NSNA)
Web site http://www.nsna.org
555 W. 57th Street, New York, NY 10019
Telephone: (212) 581-2211 (9AM—5PM Eastern Time); Fax: (212) 581-2368; e-mail: nsna@nsna.org

Nursing Spectrum
Web site http://www.nursingspectrum.com; (Circulation) Telephone: (800) 770-0866

Metro Edition: 2353 Hassell Road Suite 110, Hoffman Estates, IL 60195-2102; Telephone: (847) 839-1700

Greater Chicago / Tri-State Edition: 2353 Hassell Road Suite 110, Hoffman Estates, IL 60195-2102; Telephone: (847) 839-1700

New York & New Jersey Edition: 900 Merchants Concourse, Westbury, NY 11590; Telephone: (516) 222-0909; Fax: (516) 222-0131

Washington D.C. & Baltimore Edition: 803 West Broad Street #500, Falls Church, VA 22046; Telephone: (703) 237-6515; Fax: (703) 237-6299

Florida Edition: 1001 W. Cypress Creek Road #300, Ft. Lauderdale, FL 33309; Telephone: (954) 776-1455; Fax: (954) 776-1456

Philadelphia / Tri-State Edition: 2002 Renaissance Boulevard #250, King of Prussia, PA 19406; Telephone: (610) 292-8000; Fax: (610) 292-0179

New England Edition: 1050 Waltham Street # 510, Lexington, MA 02421; Telephone: (781) 863-2300; Fax: (781) 863-6277

Caregiving

Administration on Aging
Web site: http://www.aoa.dhhs.gov
330 Independence Avenue, SW, Washington, DC 20201
Telephone: (800) 677-1116 (Eldercare Locator—to find services for an older person in his or her locality); (202) 619-7501 (AoA's

National Aging Information Center, for technical information and public inquiries); Fax: (202) 260-1012

Elder Action: Action Ideas For Older persons and Their Families Caregivers, Caregiving and Home Care Workers
Web site: http://www.aoa.dhhs.gov/aoa/eldractn/caregive.html

Eldercare Locator: A WAY TO FIND COMMUNITY ASSISTANCE FOR SENIORS
Telephone: (800) 677-1116

Assisted Living Federation of America (ALFA)
Web site: http://www.alfa.org
10300 Eaton Place, Suite 400, Fairfax, VA 22030
Telephone: (703) 691-8100; Fax: (703) 691-8106
e-mail: info@alfa.org

Family Caregiver Alliance (FCA)
Web site: http://www.caregiver.org
690 Market Street, Suite 600, San Francisco, CA 94104
Telephone: (415) 434 3388; Fax: (415) 434 3508
e-mail: info@caregiver.org

Homecare Online: Profiles in Caring
Web site: http://www.nahc.org/NAHC/Val/Columns/SC10-1.html

National Family Caregivers Association (NFCA)
Web Site: http://www.nfcacares.org.
10400 Connecticut Avenue, #500 Kensington, MD 20895-3944;
Telephone: (800) 896-3650; Fax: (301) 942 2302; e-mail:
info@nfcacares.org

Printed in the United States
819500002B